Tulips

AREND JAN VAN DER HORST AND SAM BENVIE

FIREFLY BOOKS

A FIREFLY BOOK

Cataloguing in Publication Data

Horst, Arend Jan van der
Tulips : the complete guide to selecting and growing

(The gardener's library)
Includes index.
ISBN 1-55209-198-8

1. Tulips. I. Benvie, Sam. II. Title.
III. Series: The gardener's library (Toronto, Ont.).

SB413.T9H67   1998a   635.9'3432   C97-931996-X

Published in the United States in 1998 by
Firefly Books (U.S.) Inc.
P.O. Box 1338
Ellicot Station
Buffalo, NY USA
14205

Design and layout: Ton Wienbelt
Photography: Marcel Malherbe, Frank Beekers
Photo editor: fa. Onderwater
Production: TextCase
Translation: Alastair Weir for First Edition Translations Ltd.
Typesetting: Hof&Land Typografie

Printed and bound in Slovenia

98 99 00 01 6 5 4 3 2 1

Contents

Introduction

In temperate regions of North America, as in Europe, few harbingers of spring are as welcome after the gray days of late winter as the bright and varied colors of the tulip. While there are certainly earlier flowers, none exceeds the sheer exuberance of the tulip, which remains, for many, the quintessential flower of spring.

Perhaps because of its popularity, as well as the ease and dependability with which its well-known hybrid types produce their bloom, the tulip is often regarded as a common, if not overused, plant. Unfortunately, in North America, its use as a garden plant is limited to early season mass displays of vivid color, a welcome—albeit brief—prelude to the main event that comes with the flowers of late spring, summer and early fall.

Except among those who have traveled and observed widely or studied the history of landscape design, there is a tendency to think of the tulip as a plant without much design potential. As this book makes abundantly clear, the tulip is immensely rich in history and has played a role in the varied human pursuits of war, conquest, politics, economics and horticulture. At times it has held up a mirror to both human virtue and vice. Only a handful of the plants of beauty can rival its varied connections to Western history. Like the rose, the tulip has attained its ubiquitous success largely because of the ways in which people have interacted culturally over the past millennium, from the distant days of the high Crusades, to the tulipomania of the seventeenth century to the present day; from the high steppes of central Asia to the verdant fields of Montecello to the dazzling displays at Keukenhof. To look at the history of the tulip is to look at the clash and quest of human culture.

It is not surprising, then, to find that throughout the course of Western history, as cultures have developed and redefined their sense of place in the world, and as landscape design has consequently changed, the use and appreciation of plants, the tulip included, has changed, developed and become more refined. The tulip finds a fitting place in such varied historical designs as those of the Moors and Moguls, as well as those of colonial New England and the English cottage garden. Tracing the history of various landscape designs reveals ways in which the tulip can be used, other than the current practices of mass planting or temporary fill-ins.

This book is a richly varied historical source of information for designing with the tulip in mind. It contains a useful summary of the various types of tulips, the time and circumstances of their discovery and many visual examples showing tulips in the context of large comprehensive designs.

Whether or not you actually grow tulips, even the most casual reading will leave you with different and exciting new ways to look at tulips, the favored flowers of spring.

Sam Benvie

The Tulip: An Asiatic Harbinger of Spring

T he origin of the tulip is not linked to any single place, nor is it possible to indicate any one area from which this fascinating flower spread. It is found in the wild in North Africa, southern Italy, southern France, Turkey, China, Japan, and Korea. The tulip made a long journey before it finally reached our gardens. In an apparently mysterious way the bulb, hidden in the ground, has succeeded in crossing steppes, surmounting mountain ranges and passing over barren deserts.

Above: *Tulipa biflora* 'maxima' is a low-growing wild tulip, which develops long leaves. It flowers early and on slightly richer soil the flowers should return annually.

Right: *Tulipa kaufmanniana* 'Jeantine'.

Like most self-propagating plants, the tulip, too, has a secret vehicle: seed. This is formed naturally through the pollination of the densely grouped bulbs, and is carried by the wind in enormous clouds of dust, still common in countries like China or North Africa. Personal experience has shown that at least once every year the cars parked beside the Amsterdam canals are covered with a thin layer of desert sand from the Sahara. The yellow sand is washed away by the rain, and eventually the seeds disappear with the rainwater.

Tulip seeds may also have been effectively spread from place to place, as are many other seeds, by birds, who eat them and later cast them out in their droppings. Seeds may cling to the fur of wild animals and then fall to the ground elsewhere, where they can germinate. This means of transport, provided by nature via, for example, horses and camels, could

Tulips in a naturally occurring undergrowth seem to be part of the wild flora.

Here *Tulipa* 'Peach Blossom', a double early tulip.

explain the flower's remarkable journey, over centuries, around half our globe at an average latitude of 40°. This parallel runs from Korea, Japan and China through Uzbekistan, Tajikistan, and Turkmenistan, on to Armenia and Turkey.

Of all the possible birthplaces of the tulip, Central Asia can undoubtedly be considered to have the greatest claim. Somewhere in the Chinese province of Tienshan and in the southernmost part of the former Soviet Union, Pamir Alai, lies, as is now indisputably established, the cradle of the tulip.

Above: *Tulipa greigii* **'Mary Ann'**.

Right: *Tulipa bakeri* **'Lilac Wonder'**.

The tulip travels through Asia

Dissemination probably took place in three distinct directions. In the first the tulip traveled south, to the fertile fields and damp marshy banks of Kashmir. In the same direction it also crossed the Himalayas. The tulip was known in the gardens of India and was often planted as a favorite spring flower. Living reminders are still to be found, particularly in the still extant gardens of the Mogul emperors, who in the summer sought the cool of their pleasure gardens on the banks of the Kashmir lakes.

The tulip also traveled north, to Mongolia and Priblakhash. Here, however, nature itself produced a frontier. The long-lasting frost, penetrating deep into the ground, made it impossible for tulip bulbs to protect themselves from freezing in the earth.

That is after all the secret of the tulip. The bulb

withdraws underground to protect itself in summer from the scorching heat on the steppes and in the valleys, and in winter to profit from an insulating layer of earth. That is why tulip bulbs can survive in regions where the top layer of soil is frozen in winter. The more deeply concealed bulb is not damaged by the hard frozen ground. When the soil freezes, the water in it expands, damaging the bulb. Although the tulip, like many other bulbs, has a thick layer of protective material around its core, a long, hard frost can still destroy the bulb. This is why the cold frontier above the 40° parallel has always been the northernmost limit of the tulip's distribution.

A third direction of dissemination ran westward from Central Asia into Asia Minor. The tulip came to Europe from Asia Minor via the Balkans: first to Italy and from there to France and Spain. From Spain the tulip traveled to the western and central

This low-growing, early flowering I. *kaufmanniana* 'Giuseppe Verdi' is suitable for the perennial garden, the patio in troughs and pots, and on the balcony. Strong winds or drafts are no problem with the low-growing varieties.

parts of North Africa and finally found an insurmountable barrier in the Sahara, which was too wide for the tulip seeds to be sent across.

The original species of tulip

Tulipa kaufmanniana, T. greigii, T. fosteriana, T. praestans and *T. eichleri* are all found as wild varieties, which have managed to distribute themselves independently over wide tracts without any human intervention, and have been of inestimable value to us.

The Unknown Tulip

T*he tulip was first treasured as a plant of exceptional beauty in the Turkish empire of the fifteenth and sixteenth centuries.*

The great Ottoman Empire, as it was then called, at that time included not only the whole of Asia Minor, but also Armenia, Azerbaijan, Syria, the Sinai peninsula, Mesopotamia, Egypt, Palestine, and North Africa. Warlike but garden-loving sultans wielded the scepter there.

The bulbs from Asia Minor and the Far East so beloved of Ottoman sultans have not yet betrayed their secret, though many varieties have been propagated by pollination.

Right: Triumph tulip 'Attila' and mixed Darwin hybrids.

A large part of the Caucasus and the regions around the Black Sea were also part of this empire and many of the wild tulips so beloved by the Turkish sultans were found there.

The Crimea was wrested from the Khan, the contemporary ruler of the Tartars, by transshipping an enormous army to the port of Kaffa, where the Tartars were defeated without quarter.
The wild blooms which the Ottoman army commanders took back to their ruler were called after this port and were known as *Café Lalé*. *Café* was the indication that they had been found near Kaffa. These tulips were taken to the new capital of the Ottoman empire, Istanbul, formerly known as Constantinople, which the Turks had conquered, taking it from the Christians in 1453.

The supreme ruler Mehmet el Fatih (1451–81), also known as Mohammed II and as the Conqueror, was a great lover of gardens. He was particularly interested in tulips: he had them tracked down in the countries he ruled, regardless of expense and trouble, and transferred to gardens specially laid out for them, in which he could enjoy them each spring with the ladies of his harem. His love of both conquest and gardens was shared by his successors, for whom tulips remained an abiding interest.

These Darwin hybrids are called 'Pink Impression', indicating that this strong variety harmonizes well with all white, blue, and deep purple colors. D. W. Lefebre produced the first Darwin hybrids in the 1940s.

Suleiman the Magnificent reigned from 1520 to 1566. During his reign bulbs were propagated further, leading to a diversity of variations and colors. Close attention was paid to the shape of the flower, which had to be an elongated almond shape. The stamens had to be sword-shaped and strong and sturdy. The petals could touch each other and the stalk should hold the flowerhead upright. The three innermost stamens should be closer together than the outer ones, while the pistil should be invisible. This resulted in the search for elongated tulips with petals tapering to a point.

Further refinements of the tulip had been the object of search in Turkey for many centuries before the rest of the world even had any suspicion of the existence of this flower. Only much later did anyone outside Turkey hear of this mysterious, enchanting bloom,

Above: *Tulipa kaufmanniana* **'Fashion'.**

Below: *Tulipa kolpakowskiana.*

which was to be called tulip in other countries, while in Turkey itself it had become known as Café Lalé.

The limited distribution of tulips in the gardens of earlier rulers of Asia Minor and North Africa is remarkable. Nor were tulips known in Greece at least they are not described in the Greece of Dioscorides and Theophrastus. Nowhere do either of them mention this flower, although they do refer, for instance, to the *Leucojum*. Theophrastus describes this flower as a snowflake, *leukoion* in Greek.

The first illustration of *Tulipa* to appear in western Europe was a splendid picture of a tulip, with many leaves and a bulb with roots, in Petrus Andrea Matthiolus's book *Commentarii secundo aucti in Libre sexpedacii Dioscoridis anazarbei de medica materia*, which was published in 1559. The practice of publishing in Latin meant that the text could be read in all civilized parts of Europe. It is remarkable that in this book Matthiolus gave no description of the tulip illustrated, though he did in his next book, the *Historia Plantarum* of 1565.

Two yellow-flowered tulips are also mentioned in a book by the botanist Mathias de l'Obel: *Tulipa sylvestris* and *T. australis* from the Middle East.

However, long before these scholars, the Flemish diplomat Ogier Ghiselin de Busbecq had written of the tulips he saw at the court of Suleiman I, sultan of Turkey.

The first tulip for the Flemish ambassador

Suleiman possessed splendid gardens not only in Istanbul, but in what is now called Edirne (up to the sixteenth century Adrianople), in Turkey-in-Europe. It was in these extensive gardens that Ogier Ghiselin de Busbecq, ambassador of the Austrian emperor Ferdinand I, in 1554 saw for the first time tulips blooming in large numbers and varieties.

The Turks also called tulips *tulipan*, derived from *dalban*, meaning a turban, and this is how de Busbecq described their flowers in a letter to Charles de l'Ecluse, a botanist in Vienna. In 1573 Charles de l'Ecluse, better known as Clusius, had been appointed prefect of the Imperial Physic Garden by Emperor Maximilian II. De busbecq's enthusiastic description aroused de l'Ecluse's curiosity.

Above: *Tulipa acuminata* gives an idea of the favorite variety of sultans like Suleiman the Magnificent. The pointed petals reach upward on a tall graceful stem.

In his function as head of this garden full of medicinal plants, established in Vienna, he received the first tulip bulbs and seeds from de Busbecq. There was also a description of how the bulbs were planted and propagated in the sultan's garden.

De Busbecq's letters have survived and are included in the *Epistolae de Rebus Turcicis*. He called his discovery *Tulipa Turcarum*, the tulip of the Turks. That was in fact an incorrect description. The birthplace of the tulip was Central Asia.

This fact, however, emerged only in the twentieth century, mainly as a result of the activities of the Van Tubergen company of Lisse in the Netherlands. It is thanks to this world-famous firm of bulb growers that a number of botanists was sent to all parts of Asia where it was suspected that there might be interesting bulbs, particularly wild species of tulip. This is therefore a very recent scientific discovery,

which detracts in no way from de Busbecq's effort to provide his friend Clusius with interesting botanical specimens.

Tulips now bloomed in Vienna, but they were not the first tulips imported into western Europe. That honor fell in 1559 to the banker Johannes Heinrich Herwart from Augsburg.

News of their blooming was made known to a few interested botanists, resulting initially in a visit from the Swiss botanist Conrad Gensher to the Augsburg garden. Gensher described his visit in an "Omnibus" and in it told of the flower, which he also called *Tulipa Turcarum*. His account of it was included in *De hortis germaniae liber recens,* published by Valerius Cordus in 1561.

How these tulips reached Augsburg is not known. It is possible that Venetian merchants knew what prices tulips commanded in the Ottoman empire, particularly the special varieties. They must often have been commissioned by the well-known banker Herwart to hunt out special plants for his garden. If this was a common practice, tulips were undoubtedly to be found in many more gardens belonging to prosperous western Europeans trading with Venice. However, none of this is properly documented, so that the Augsburg garden remains the acknowledged first.

One remarkable discovery must be included in this narrative. In *Tulips*, by Tom Lodewijk, the author reports an exciting discovery during the Second World War, after the bombing of Coventry Cathedral. A wall painting was discovered there which had never been exposed before, showing a Madonna and Child, surrounded by tulips. This fifteenth-century illustration is therefore the earliest known picture of the tulip in western Europe, except, of course, for representations on the many textiles and tiles which had already arrived earlier from Persia and the Ottoman empire.

It can only be wondered at that it was not until the sixteenth century that the flower appeared in the gardens of western Europe. The most obvious reason lies in the severe punishments imposed on the Turkish gardeners, harem guards, and the residents of the harem, if they stole one of the tulips from the sultan's garden. No flower was allowed to leave the garden, let alone a bulb ... So the tulip, unfortunately with great success, was kept secret for the private pleasure of the lord and the ladies of the harem.

It also remains remarkable that tulip bulbs had not been imported earlier from China with other merchandise via the silk route. Perhaps in the regions where it occurred naturally, the tulip was thought "too ordinary," so that the potential interest in it abroad was not appreciated.

Perhaps, too, its relatively short flowering period was a reason to assume that it had no commercial value. If it had been known how great the popularity of this bulb was to become in the western world,

Two double tulips, 'Mount Tacoma' and 'Carlton', of a bright red color. According to the "book," the first of these tulips is late-flowering and the second flowers early; here is the result if there is an exception to the rule.

'Johann Strauss' is a *kaufmanniana* tulip originally from Central Asia. Van Tubergen crossed this early flowering variety of tulip with *greigii* and *fosteriana*; as a result a large number of new hybrids came on the market.

then undoubtedly tulips would have reached the West much earlier on the backs of camels, donkeys, and horses.

The tulip in Islamic culture

What the gardens with their tulips must have looked like can be traced fairly accurately. In western Europe the tulip became known as an ornamental plant only in the second half of the sixteenth century; most of the first gardens to display them must therefore have been in the Orient.

Unlike in Christian culture, no human personages or gods could be portrayed in Islamic architecture, sculpture, or painting. The western, central, and northern Europeans made images of saints and venerated them, but this was not permitted by Islamic law. In other religions, such as Chinese and

Japanese Confucianism and then later in Hinduism, representations of gods and saints were allowed. Islamic art was consequently in a unique position. Geometric shapes such as octagons, circles, ovals, rectangles, and all the shapes and patterns derived from them, were of course allowed, and these were, perhaps through necessity, developed into sublime decorative styles. Plants, too, could serve as sources of inspiration, among them roses and tulips. The domes of mosques are marvels of architecture, and great artistic skill and sophistication are also demonstrated by the finely decorated tiles. In Spain, the Alhambra in Granada has alabaster pillars of rare elegance supporting walls of the lightest filigree plasterwork, acting as eaves for the halls behind them. These halls have marble floors, through which small streams of water are led. The complex of many inner courts is sublime in its simplicity. In the

Left: Many 'Duc van Tol' tulips are red, but there are also violet variants of this old variety of tulip, which belongs to the single early-flowering groups. This is 'Duc van Tol Scarlet'.

Generalife, the palace built close to the Alhambra by the Moors in the thirteenth century, they offered room to walk. They are walled areas, built in a specific order. First was the hall of public audience, then the private hall of audience in which the sultan held court, followed by the private apartments of the sultan and of the harem, while some distance from this large, still perfectly preserved palace was a private palace, a kind of summer residence for the sultan, built slightly higher up the hillside. Here, too, gardens – flower and water gardens – were laid out.

CHAPTER 3

Garden Design in the Ottoman Empire

T here are three sources to which anyone wanting to know more about the design and cultivation of the Oriental garden culture, begun in the fifteenth century and continued for hundreds of years, can turn. First, there are the splendid paintings in which these gardens are portrayed. Second, there are the carpets, now known generally as "Persian carpets," inspired by the blossoming inner courts. Third, there are the few surviving gardens, of which those of the Alhambra and the Generalife in Spain represent the peak of excellence.

Above: Tulips can also be grown in pots, preferably buried in the soil or, if indoors, somewhere cool and dark.

Right: Fringed tulips are a real treasure, such as this 'Fringed Beauty'.

Yet fine gardens have also been preserved in India, laid out by the Mogul emperors. Particularly in Kashmir, but also elsewhere in India, these centuries-old gardens can be found, designed and planted completely in the style of the Persian–Turkish gardens. The layout often followed a fixed pattern. A long straight path ran as a central axis through the garden area that could be seen from the palace or pavilion. This paved path was interrupted by a pool, often with a fountain.

The pool could be round, square, rectangular, or octagonal. Near the pool a path was often laid out at

The Darwin hybrid 'Apeldoorn' is a popular flower for cutting, but also gives a fine patch of color in the garden. It flowers for a long time, its shape radiates power, and the color is cheerful. It is one of the best-known Dutch tulips.

right angles to the central path, leading left and right into the garden. The cross created in this way was meant to symbolize heaven, which Muslim believers at the time thought was intersected by the four greatest rivers known to them: the Euphrates, the Tigris, the Nile and the Ganges. Using the cross pattern of paths the faithful created the same pattern in the garden which they later hoped to meet in heaven. The garden as a representation of paradise is the constantly recurring theme of Arabic–Persian gardens. The cross of paths was often created in the form of narrow water channels. Sometimes only the central axis was laid out as a waterway. Splendid examples of this are the Generalife in Spain, and in India the Taj Mahal with its long pool. To close off the end of the garden there was a choice of several possibilities. There might be cypresses leaning

toward each other. Four, six or eight cypresses were planted around an area sited at the end of the central axis, and the tops of the cypresses were curved toward each other until they touched. This created an arbour of greenery. A cypress arbor of this kind can be admired in the villa El Chapiz in Granada. Roses, with their gorgeous scent, have now been planted near it, and there is room to sit under the arbor. From the shadow of the arch of cypresses, which only allow a little sun or light through, people might look out at the garden, geometrically divided by box hedges, giving it a strict rhythmical appearance.

A second possibility was a covered seating area, which could vary from a kiosk-like building to a splendid sample of the architect's art. This was done at the Generalife, where a storey was even built above the arches of the ground floor, so that the flower garden

Above: 'Jeantine', a tulip 8 in (20 cm) high.

Below: *Tulipa* 'Attila' was introduced in 1945.

could be admired from above. In Indian gardens, too, where this idea was developed with great refinement, these pavilions often extended upward with the top story sometimes covered over and sometimes open to the air. In all the roofed pavilions the seating area was covered with fine hand-made carpets. These carpets could be interpreted as representations of gardens. People wanted to hold on to the rich colors of the glory of flowers from their gardens. The flowers were translated into silk or wool and so preserved in the carpets. Brilliant paradise gardens have been immortalized in carpets, in which the division of the garden into areas for planting and areas for walking can be seen, with the water flowing down the center.

The tulip appears in many carpets, though it is sometimes only identifiable through its color and shape by connoisseurs.

Above: *Tulipa* **'Peach Blossom'.**

Inset: A famous Parrot tulip: 'Black Parrot'.

Almonds and cypresses

In the formally ordered gardens of the Ottoman empire, flowers were used in various ways. Flowering climbers provided walls, pavilions, and pathways with beautiful foliage and sweet-scented flowers. In addition flowers, including tulips, were planted in pots.

After they had finished flowering, the tulips were replaced by later flowering plants.

Trees had their place, as can be seen from pictures of Persian, Turkish, and Indian gardens. There was always almond blossom there, which with peach blossom and the tulip, was regarded as the harbinger of spring. The almond was also the symbol of new life, as it was thought to be the first tree to flower in the garden. The cypress, on the other hand, symbolized death, not to be regarded as a daunting

Left: 'Black Parrot' forms a dark, mysterious color contrast with pink, or even more refined, cream-colored flowers of other tulips, Christmas roses, or shrubs.

Right: 'Marilyn' is a lily-flowered tulip, which is particularly suitable for use in larger groups.

prospect, but as the beginning of life in paradise. A cypress cannot be sawn down near to the ground if it is to be rejuvenated or shortened. It does not then grow any more, but dies and withers.

In paintings these two trees are often depicted in their splendor beside figures sitting or strolling in the garden: the dark vertical shape of the cypress and the gentle pink blossom of the almond. That bulbs should be planted near these trees as a spring welcome goes without saying.

Triumph Tulip 'Aureola' has the colors so popular in Indian gardens: orange, yellow, and red. In India they bloom in late summer with marigolds, red salvias, and yellow-red gazanias in the hot eastern sun.

Pomegranates, oranges, peaches, figs, date palms, and pears were also cultivated. Particularly in India much of this horticultural art has been preserved – a source of inspiration for anyone interested in this ancient horticulture which can still so easily be utilized today.

It might be an idea for the internationally famous garden complexes which are renowned for their collections of garden styles, such as the Keukenhof in the Netherlands, Longwood Gardens in Pennsylvania, or Wisley Gardens in Britain, to add an Ottoman garden to their display. It would show tulip lovers how tulips were first cherished. Perhaps a Turkish garden of this kind would be a better model for the present-day small garden, surrounded by its hedges, than the wide landscape gardens exhibited, for example, at the Keukenhof. It is difficult to imitate a park landscape in a small private garden!

In the Moorish tradition

For more than 700 years the major part of Spain and the whole of Portugal were under the rule of Moorish sultans. They had invaded Spain across the Straits of Gibraltar in 711 and had defeated the native population, who stood no chance against the fast Arab horses and the Muslim warriors with their curved scimitars.

The whole of Spanish and Portuguese architecture is strongly influenced by Moorish building traditions, and years after the Moors were defeated in 1492 by Ferdinand and Isabella, king and queen of Spain and

Portugal, after a long and bloody struggle, their style of architecture continued to be accepted and applied everywhere in both countries. A hybrid style emerged, which made use of Moorish arches for arcades, gateways, doors, and structural arches in roofs. Decorative motifs in brick or stucco, and tiles to decorate dwellings, were part of it. These tiles form an enduring reminder of the tradition, originating in Asia Minor, of enlivening walls with their illustrations. Throughout Portugal many of these tiled walls can still be seen in perfect condition, including those in the palace at Sintra, near Lisbon, where a summer palace built by the sultans for their pleasure has been preserved intact. There are inner courts with walls tiled in green, yellow, blue, and white, and tiled floors.

Palms, mimosa, and orange trees spill their branches

Above: 'Mrs J.T. Scheepers'.

Below: Wild *Tulipa greigii*.

over the walls which always enclose the inner courts. There are also many basins of water. Water drips into these basins from stone or marble ornaments, surrounded by flowerpots. Along a wall grows a rose, and its many blooms spread their sweet scent.

Throughout Portugal these examples of Arabic–Persian architecture can be found, as they can in Spain, in such towns as Seville, Cordoba, and Granada. The old towns in both countries are built entirely according to the Arabic tradition, often with a citadel at the highest point, where the garrison could keep watch and where the local representatives of the supreme power could take refuge whenever necessary. Below lie the small twisting alleys along which the tall houses stand with their shops and workrooms for the craftsmen. Anyone who wanders through the old part of Seville or Cordoba can still see the perfectly preserved old town centers with their courts full of flowers, now with bougainvillaea, climbing jasmine, roses, and oleanders. Orange and lemon trees grow luxuriantly there, as do geraniums. These courts provide an unchanged picture of the gardener's art since the days of the Arabs. The many palaces they built have also been preserved. In the Alcazars, such as the one in Seville, it is still possible to see how the sultans lived in their large palaces. The palaces are also splendid demonstrations of how brickwork can be combined with stone masonry.

The gardens are mysterious, with fine reflective pools, clattering fountains, palms, roses, ferns, and

'Dreaming Maid' is the appropriate name of this Triumph Tulip.

everywhere seats and pavilions covered with *azuelos*, the colored tiles.

Casa Pilatus

Delightful, too, is the Casa Pilatus which has been preserved entirely in the Moorish style. There, too, you find inner courts with arcades, so that you can sit or walk in the shade when the summer sun is too hot. Brick courts, splendid tiled retreats, are entirely surrounded by walls, and the great central garden. This is laid out in accordance with the Islamic or Arabic–Persian principle with two paths crossing each other, dividing it into four large segments. In the center at the crossing of the main paths is a fountain, which consists of a marble water basin placed on a high pedestal. Water flows from a pipe hidden in the middle of the basin, flows on over the rim, and falls in thin drops into a marble basin on a

Above left: This richly variegated group is called Fritillaria.

Below left: *Tulipa pulchella violacea* grows no higher than 4 in (10 cm). *T. pulchella* have purple flowers.

Right: One of the most delicate colors is that of the tulip 'Apricot Beauty', introduced in 1953. This single early tulip mixes well with all white, greeny yellow, and soft cream-colored flowers.

stand below. The water finally flows away again through the garden, irrigating the plants in the great flower beds. The whole garden is rich in shadows, full of mystery and cool.

Such a garden would be quite unsuitable for tulips. These can after all only survive in full sunlight and only then go on flowering from year to year.

The tulip requires full sun

In the short period of the tulip's flowering, but particularly when the leaves have reached their full development, two important steps must be taken to ensure their survival. First of all the progeny has to be protected. Bees take care of pollination. Seeds are formed, and when the seedcases and the seeds mature and ripen, they spring open so that the seeds can fall to the ground. Then follows the process of germination and a small flower is formed. The roots produced by this kind of small bulb shrink down from the top, drawing the bulb downwards. It ends up some $2\frac{1}{2}$–4 in (6–10 cm) below the surface, where it is completely protected from the sun and from drying out. Next the existing tulip, while in leaf and in flower, ensures the nourishment of the bulb which, while buried in the ground, has already provided the food for the bloom and foliage. In the short time that they flourish above ground, the leaves provide its nourishment. When the leaves wither, this nourishment is transferred to the newly formed bulb, and this bulb takes the place of the completely used-up bulb which has just finished flowering. In this way the tulip renews itself each year. For that reason good development of the foliage is essential.

In very shaded gardens tulips cannot survive, at least not planted out. They can, of course, be grown in pots which can be moved into the full sun while the tulips are in flower. After flowering, the tulips have to be planted out again in the garden where their foliage can die off. It is better to keep the plants well watered until the foliage has died off naturally, and only then to take the bulbs out of the pots, to dry them, and in the autumn to repot them in good soil. This technique also comes from Asia Minor and is standard practice in many countries around the Mediterranean.

Research suggests that in the past gardens were planted less densely. It appears that the central garden of the Alhambra palace, the Lion Court, had no, or very few plants in it.

The Alhambra, a miracle of gardening techniques
In the hot regions where the Moors laid out their gardens and built their palaces, it was necessary to irrigate the gardens. For this, irrigation and watering techniques were used which were still unknown in western Europe. Everything was done to bring sufficient water to the garden and the palace in summer, as can be seen at the Alhambra. Anyone who has visited Granada knows that the palace is built on the top of a hill, a wooded hill with winding

Tulipa kaufmanniana 'Johann Strauss' is suitable for low-growing groups with warm colors.

The *fosteriana* tulips, originating in Asia Minor, are low-growing, such as this red 'Cantata' with its brownish-green striped foliage.

roads leading up to it from the old part of the town. To get sufficient water up the hill, it had to be brought a long way from a still higher region – the Sierra Nevada. The water was led via channels and underground earthenware pipes from the mountain tops covered with eternal snow, hundreds of miles away. The meltwater was piped to the Alhambra in the summer, an example of technical skill which it would be difficult to surpass nowadays. In the gardens it could create many forms of coolness for the sultans, the ladies of their harem, and the eunuchs, the castratos who guarded the harem against unwelcome visitors.

First of all there is the long rectangular pool of the Court of Myrtles, which takes its name from the two hedges standing to left and right of the pool. Water is continually brought into the pool at both ends via

Above: This botanical tulip is remarkable for its yellow centers.

Below: *Tulipa pulchella humilis* (syn. *T. humilis*).

two round marble basins set slightly above ground level. Around it are walls, to left and right, not ornamented, but overgrown with jasmine, the sweet-scented climber covered with small white flowers. The next court, Daraxa's garden, has numerous trees, including cypresses, with, in the center, a water container on a pedestal from which water drips into a basin below. Here you find red salvias, the richly colored flowers of summer.

In the third court is the lion fountain. This fountain, which is not in fact at all appropriate in a Moorish or Arabic–Persian garden, displays twelve lions whose jaws pour streams of water into a basin. It is thought that this sculpture was made by the Visigoths, who were able to call a halt to the Moorish invasion in the north of Spain and south of France. This kind of sculpture is typical of the plastic art of this almost forgotten people, who for centuries played such an important role and who produced art of a very high quality.

Water flowing from the central Lion Court connects the inner and outer courts through narrow water channels made in the floors of the rooms situated around the court. When this palace was restored fairly recently, all the flowers and the orange trees which once surrounded the fountain were removed from the now empty flower beds. It makes your fingers itch to plant the varieties of tulips there which were known to contemporaries, together with hyacinths, crocuses, scillas, and, of course, ornamental onion bulbs. In the summer there could

Pink blooms of *Tulipa humilis* in a town garden.

be annuals with the perennial Acanthus plant. In this way a sunny flower garden could be laid out, though according to Spanish art historians there has never been one there.

In the Alhambra a large garden comes next, with tall palm trees and a rather more open character than the gardens in the walled courts. Terraces are constructed at different levels, with pots filled with annuals, while cypresses, as hedges or single trees, divide the various spaces. The terraced gardens run down to a large rectangular pool with palm trees planted round it. Tall oleanders grow there, too. The pool marks the end of this fascinating garden.

Below left: The fringed tulip 'Crystal Beauty'.

Below right: An impression of 'Black Parrot'.

The Generalife

A deep ravine, pleasantly overgrown with wild trees and shrubs, separates the site of the Alhambra from another hill, which can be seen from the palace. In 1377 Mohammed Ben Al-Atimar, the sultan of the Alhambra, had his splendid summer residence built on this hill.

This palace, the Generalife, consists of various courts filled with the clatter of water. Everything here was aimed at the refinements of pleasure.

The central space consists of a long, narrow rectangular pool, which is closed in on right and left by a high wall.

At each end of it are pavilions, each of two storeys. Flowers are planted round the long pool and fine jets of water sprinkle down onto both sides from this pool.

Next to this main garden lies a second somewhat smaller one, consisting almost entirely of water. Water spouts upwards from the centrally placed pool. This is done through elevated ornaments and from the edges of the pool in a play of water that seems to be never ending. A single stair connects this water garden with a house higher up. There are channels in the balustrades of the fairly steep steps, in which water also flows – an invitation to rest your arms on the balustrade to cool your hands, and go down refreshed to the next spectacle.

A second, new garden has been laid out below, beside the existing long main garden, at a slightly lower level than the water garden. Here, too, water is used in a long channel, somewhat repetitive of what is already there, and adding a little fascination to the age-old brilliant concept of the garden. The endless ranks of standard roses planted in this new

Tulipa fosteriana **'Purissima' returns every year in this garden. This tulip fits in beautifully with the dark** *Chamaecyparis* **trunk, reminiscent of the symbolism of the cypress and the almond tree – death and renewed life. Islamic garden design combines both to illustrate their inseparable nature.**

garden provide a grateful subject for photographs and water-colors. The pots, planted with geraniums, salvias, and many other annuals, are a pleasant sight, while tall cypresses provide the garden with walls and divisions, like those seen earlier in this complex.

There are no tulips in the gardens of the Alhambra or the Generalife. Bulb experts would know what varieties were grown at the time of their conception. These gardens would perhaps be made even more fascinating by their use.

CHAPTER 4

Man As a Means of Transport: The Knight of Martena

According to tradition, starting in the eleventh century during the Crusades against the local rulers in Palestine, many of the combatants brought back bulbs which had attracted their attention by their blooms. One familiar story is that of the Friesian knight of Martena, who brought back bulbs from Palestine, Turkey, Greece, and Italy to his garden in Franekeradeel in Friesland, after he had been on the Crusade. This knight is interesting as an example of the many thousands of crusaders who visited these lands.

He undertook the expensive and dangerous journey to Palestine, the Holy Land, in order to free the country from the Saracens, whatever the cost. In that way he could ensure his place in heaven, a prospect which seemed to make the sacrifice worthwhile.

A formal garden with box hedges and brick paths. This white Triumph tulip 'Inzell' stands alone in its pot and reminds us of the time when tulips were worth their weight in gold.

In the garden of the knight of Martena, who lived in the twelfth century, many of his discoveries can still be admired. Among others they include the wild tulip, *Tulipa sylvestris*, with its yellow flowers. This may have been how the first *T. sylvestris* came to be planted in the far north of the Netherlands. There are other kinds of bulbs, such as *Corydalis lutea*, *Scilla*, and the botanical *Crocus tomassianum* in the spacious garden, which was redesigned in the nineteenth century in landscape, or better named, English garden style, by the garden designer Roodbaard.

In the days of the knight of Martena, the flowers would have been planted in neatly edged beds with paths of shells between them. In Friesland the sea was nearby, so broken seashells were often used in place of gravel walks in gardens along the coast.

There were probably box hedges around the flower beds in which, after the bulbs were over, perennials and annuals bloomed. There were pollarded trees – apples, pears, or limes – in an enclosed flower garden. Fences of plaited osiers were covered with roses, honeysuckle, and espaliered fruit trees, forming an airy frame for the colorful flower gardens. Often in such gardens there was also a covered, shady walk through standards and arches of oak. Sometimes these were grown into arbors, or hedges were trained over them. Windows were cut in the hedges, giving views of the magnificent flower garden.

Near this twelfth-century keep the author planted these 'Queen of Night' tulips in what becomes an exuberant border during the summer months.

"Manor house" plants spread through the Netherlands

It is not only in the Netherlands that one meets bulbs brought back by crusading knights, but in many countries of Europe. Throughout western Europe, volunteers enlisted to fight against the blasphemous – in their eyes – seizure of Palestine by the Muslims. England, France, Germany, the Low Countries, Italy, and Spain supplied lay knights, military orders, and many others, who voluntarily, or under more or less pressure from their feudal lords, journeyed to distant Asia Minor. On horseback and later perhaps by ass and camel, they traveled past the endless steppes and through fertile valleys, and in the spring admired the bulbs growing there in the high sun, hyacinths, daffodils, crocuses, scillas, and tulips. The knight of Martena's bulbs were highly valued and admired by his family, friends, and other guests. Their natural demand for these flowers led to the spread of bulbs through the connections of noble families.

In the Netherlands, among country houses and castles along the River Vecht, between Utrecht and Amsterdam, these bulbs are encountered in large quantities. In other areas where noble families lived, these "stinse" or "manor house" plants, as they were called in the Netherlands, appeared.

The term *"stinse plant"* is derived from the knight of Martena. He lived in a noble manor house, a fortified house, now used as a county hall. In Friesland these manor houses are called *stinse*, literally meaning a stone house. The flowers coming from these Friesian *stinses* were therefore called *stinse plants*. There is some confusion, as the name is not always used only for the plants originally brought from Asia Minor. The spread of bulbs occurred through circles of families and friends, and this was also the case in the other countries that had sent crusaders on their holy expedition.

This double late tulip is called 'Angelique' and it can be recommended to any lover of delicate and subtle colors. It should not be put too close to tulips or other bulbs in strongly dominant colors; they risk killing its effect.

CHAPTER 5

Botanic Gardens in Europe

The first botanic garden in Europe was established in Padua in 1542, and it was entirely laid out for study and research to the design of the university. This garden can still be seen in its original state. Of course, rich Egyptians, Mesopotamians, and Romans had gardens full of exotic plants, some brought from distant lands. But the special significance of Padua is that here was a university which appreciated the importance of a botanic garden for study. The garden in Padua has existed for five centuries without alteration – a small miracle. For all these centuries students have been able to come here to learn and examine the plants set out in their small neat beds. Whether there were also tulips here in the fifteenth century is not known. There were certainly grasses and special plants from distant countries such as tomatoes and potatoes, which were studied here for the first time. It was at that time that their nutritional value became apparent, and the potato, that thickened root from the Andes, which had been the staple food of Indians from time immemorial, began its victorious career.

In the sixteenth and seventeenth centuries variegated and striped tulips were popular, and they were often painted. Here the Triumph tulip 'Lucky Strike', which goes well with dark ranunculas.

The design of the Padua garden is magnificent. You enter the botanic garden through a circular wall, running all around the perimeter. Long paths lead from entrances in this circular wall to a central point where a fountain tumbles. Circular paths are laid out encircling the round water basins, dividing the space into ever increasing larger rings. Paths radiating from the fountain divide these circular sections into beds in which flowers are planted. Around this central part lie other gardens, filled with plants chosen thematically. There are gardens for herbs, grasses, vegetables, and many ornamental plants. This garden in Padua attracts visitors from far and near, and offers not only medicinal plants, but other nutritional and ornamental plants for study. It was already world famous in the sixteenth century for its beauty as well as for its research facilities.

Above: *Tulipa acuminata* grows to a height of 12 in (30 cm).

Below: *Tulipa kaufmanniana* 'Jeantine' is low-growing.

Clusius's garden in Leiden

Clusius's much simpler garden in Leiden was established in 1592, after he had left his physic garden in Vienna. The Austrian city had entered an uncertain and dangerous period with the religious troubles, so that Clusius's appointment as prefect of the renowned Hortus Botanicus of the northern university was more than welcome to him. He did not take his whole collection of plants with him, but did take many specialties, including his collection of tulips. He probably left some tulips behind in Vienna, but must have ensured that he could take with him a well-cataloged supply of bulbs, which were not too obvious in his baggage. Could he have smuggled them? It is difficult to imagine that Emperor Maximilian, his employer in Vienna, would

have been happy to see an important collection of plants depart with his prefect.

In 1601 Clusius wrote his *Rariorum Plantarium Historia* in which he recorded that traders in Vienna had offered him tulips. These traders probably came from Constantinople, and they called the tulips they offered *Café Lalé* and *Cavalé Lalé*. The early-flowering *Café Lalé* bulbs come from the Crimea on the Black Sea, the *Cavalé Lalé* from a port on the Aegean to the east of the present-day Salonica. It is

Two Triumph tulips: 'Blenda' and 'Edith Eddy'. Both have long stems, and are therefore suitable for planting between fast-growing perennials which hide the foliage when the tulips have finished flowering.

assumed that the tulips from the Crimea were *Tulipa schrenki*, since they are still common wild tulips there, flowering on the low hills of the Caucasus and also along the eastern shores of the Caspian Sea. There they grew wild in various colors, and wild white, pink, wine-red, orange, and lilac *T. schrenki* can still be found. The tulips offered to Clusius by traders who called them *Cavalé Lalé* probably came from Macedonia. Wild late-flowering tulips are still found there along the banks of the River Vadar.

Clusius was interested in *Tulipae* and we must assume that they were included in his growing collection of tulips. By experimenting with the pollination of one species with another, and by crossing the varieties within a single species, Clusius himself had built up a respectable range before moving to Leiden.

Above left: Triumph tulip 'New Design' in separate ragged rows.

Above right: 'Abu Hassan' is a brightly colored tulip suitable for old-fashioned arrangements.

Clusius's influence

Clusius guarded his bulbs carefully, and that may well be the reason for a high brick wall being built around his botanic garden in Leiden, which is still almost unchanged from its original seventeenth-century form. He cherished his Turkish tulips, showing them off to other botanists and to prominent local citizens. Tulips began to attract attention. That the prefect guarded his plants well is apparent from the various anecdotes which circulated about his enthusiasm for them. One story shows Clusius as a wise man, who also allowed other

Above: This single late tulip is named after the seventeenth-century painter Judith Leyster.

Below: *Tulipa pulchella* comes in many colors.

interested botanists to benefit from his small stock of bulbs. A second version gives another aspect of clusius's "unselfish" love for his tulips. Because of the fame his tulips had gained locally, he was asked time and again to part with some of his bulbs, which produced such wonderful flowers. The prefect, quite aware of the value of his treasure, consistently refused. Did he perhaps think that the asking price was determined by the supply? The prices offered went higher and higher, because in this version of the story no one was allowed to share in the botanist's precious possession – they might do so by looking, but not by buying. The fame of his collection grew so much that the prices offered climbed to unbelievable heights. But nothing could soften Clusius's heart. He waited, and was

A favorite for the wildflower garden: _Tulipa tarda_, which also looks very good in old terracotta pots. When these tulips are grown in pots, the bulbs must be dug out and kept dry over winter.

perhaps already secretly counting his profit, when in one disastrous night it was not a storm that destroyed his blooms, it was not mice that devoured his treasures, but a criminal, lusting after money, who skil fully dug up virtually all his bulbs and got away with them over the wall. Who it was remains a mystery. A known fact, however, is that after Clusius's time the trade in bulbs, particularly tulips, flourished. It was to Clusius's great credit that he simultaneously stimulated pleasure in cultivating the bulbs with a delight in looking at them, and the opportunity to make a profit from them. After the theft, Clusius in his disappointment turned away from further experiments with tulips, but went ahead with his extensive collections of other plants. In this he was successful; his university garden was the first of its kind in the Netherlands, and it soon attracted scientists from many countries.

Various other botanic gardens followed, notably the Hortus Botanicus in Amsterdam, founded by rich citizens, mainly merchants. Its most famous curator was Commelin, who benefited from the presence in his city of the headquarters of the East India Company, enabling him to acquire many exotic tropical and sub-tropical plants. The botanic garden in Harderwijck has, alas, disappeared, while that in Utrecht has been moved to another site.

A hortus with strange and exotic plants became a necessity for any self-respecting university town. It was a place the students could study plants: in the first instance medicinal plants, but later also other

special plants which could be useful for food or decoration. Tulips inevitably came into this category, with their fame spreading as an oriental rarity, for which reason they were given raised flower-beds, guaranteeing good drainage in wet winter weather. In Clusius's garden special beehives were sited to guarantee the pollination of, among other plants, its tulips. New varieties were also grown from seed, including some with striped flowers. For a long time growers were at a loss to understand why it was not possible to grow plants similar to the parent plant from the seed of these striped tulips. Not until the twentieth century was it discovered that a virus, a form of disease, was responsible for the stripes on the petals.

Clusius called these striped tulips "broken" tulips and described very accurately how the petals are affected. The virus affects the color, which then

Above left: In the background is the tulip 'Green Spot', a *viridiflora* tulip.

Above right: A favorite is the lily-flowered tulip 'White Triumphator'.

disappears. The remaining stripes of color, or in less serious infections, the white stripes in the plain area of color, produce a broken colored surface. In the seventeenth and eighteenth centuries, Dutch tulip growers sought long and hard for a way to grow these highly treasured and very expensive blooms with a broken or striped appearance as a true species. It became possible to cultivate them only when it was discovered that a piece of an infected bulb could be introduced into a sound bulb. When we see how often these tulips are portrayed in old botanical prints, paintings, and water-colors – far

more frequently than the healthy tulips to which preference is now given – we can understand why all the seventeenth- and eighteenth-century bulb growers did their utmost to be able to offer stocks of bulbs capable of producing these striped flowers. Money was no object, so that with the limited supply, exorbitant profits were made from them.

The secret of the striped tulip revealed

In 1901 Takami, a Japanese scientist, discovered that a beetle played an important part in transmitting the virus which caused broken tulips. Four kinds of virus were involved, not all of which were always present in the same tulip. Sometimes there was only one virus, and sometimes several, so that different symptoms resulted. The bulb institute in Lisse, the Netherlands, carried out experiments on the virus. Animals were exposed to it, but came to no harm. An animal could produce antibodies, as could man. A tulip could not, any more than could other plants which succumbed to the disease. As a result, tulip fields are now always sited in open country, without any other vegetation. Since the insect can establish itself and survive only on plants, trees, bushes, or hedges, sites free of these are chosen. In this way the spread of this very damaging disease can be prevented. By rotating bulb fields annually and leaving them fallow for two years in between, there is little opportunity for the insect to become established.

These are important developments, but the absence of the beautiful striped tulips still leaves a gap. It is perhaps a pity that somewhere cannot be found, quite separate from the other bulb-growing areas, where these diseased tulips can be grown. The customer is king, after all. And striped tulips should certainly be included in bouquets produced to represent or illustrate historical events. Fortunately there are some good replacements: healthy striped tulips and other special varieties.

Growing tulips in pots has been fashionable for centuries. Here is the single late tulip 'Demeter', which can first be placed in a cold frame until the tips show above ground, and then grown on in full light in a warmer temperature.

Parrot tulips

These splendid baroque-looking tulips are shunned by some, but highly valued by many flower arrangers. The striped petals, with their scalloped edges, the free shapes of the large petals, the frothy total effect of the flower, make this tulip suitable for mid-seventeenth-century bouquets as well as for extravagant super-modern ones. In Christian Tortu's flower shop near the Odéon in Paris parrot tulips are a frequent feature. A single tulip of this kind in a bamboo vase, or a few cut short in a Thaïs basket, produces a stunning effect and makes quite clear that this tulip is overdue for a revival. The parrot tulip was discovered in 1665. The name was probably chosen because of its variegated colors, like the varied hues of the feathers of some multicolored parakeets. It is still not known which

The Parrot tulip 'Fantasy' was introduced in 1910.

particular virus disease causes this variety. The parrot tulip can be reproduced true to species only by asexual reproduction.

CHAPTER 6

Gardens in the 17th Century

Most renaissance gardens in Europe do not differ much from each other in design. Only the geography of their site, on a flat or hilly area, or other features such as a nearby stream, a neighboring wood, or distinctive cultivation, make the gardens look quite different.

Above: 'Flaming Parrot' in a glass goblet vase.

Right: In spring tulips convincingly cheer up any garden.

French renaissance gardens

Splendid gardens were laid out in Blois between 1499 and 1514, which have been recorded in prints by Jacques du Cerceau. The gardens of the Château of Blois, the palace of the French king Louis XII and Anne of Brittany on the banks of the Loire, are laid out on a hillside on a series of terraces, leveled and supported by retaining walls. These hanging gardens were linked together by flights of steps and, where necessary, elevated bridges.

Near arched green walks, many beds were divided into geometrical shapes for flowers, vegetables, and fruit, usually with their shapes emphasized by box hedges. A selection of special plants was introduced into this pleasure garden, the hunting lodge at Blois. There were probably tulips here too;

the French court maintained good relations with the Turkish one.

The gardens at Fontainebleau, the favorite residence of Francis I who started the garden in 1528, and the Tuileries, the gardens of the royal palace of the Louvre, have been preserved in almost their original state.

There is no doubt that tulips adorned both these gardens, in pots and in borders, but there may not have been many, as it was the most expensive bloom of that period, with each bulb costing a fortune. Crispijn van de Passe, the distinguished Antwerp printer and publisher, recorded the varieties of tulips in bloom there when he traveled to Paris to record the most beautiful varieties in his prints.

Tulipa 'purissima' in a private garden.

The gardens of Frederick Henry and Amalia of Solms

Prince Frederick Henry, a lover of architecture, left his heirs four "pleasances," of which only two have survived. One of these two is Huis ten Bosch (the House in the Woods), now the official residence of Queen Beatrix of the Netherlands, a direct descendant of Frederick Henry and Amalia of Solms-Braunfels. Huis ten Bosch was designed by Pieter Post, the architect also responsible for the formal gardens, with a central axis laid out with trellises and high pedestals bearing ornamental pots.

In early spring countless tulips bloomed there, to be replaced later in the year by colorful annuals.

The walk was entirely hedged about by a green wall, meeting at the top. Windows were cut in the foliage, so that one could look out on the flowers in the sunny open court. There were also larger covered

Above: This garden combines vertical, spherical, and horizontal lines; a spot full of 'Inzell' Triumph tulips.

spaces, in which Maurice could enjoy the company of his mistress, who had been brought up a Catholic. In Protestant Holland Maurice could not marry his Catholic love from Antwerp, but he had seven children by her, all of whom later became great garden lovers. They would certainly have delighted in this garden, which has been well represented in prints. His great kitchen garden has been lost, but is still an open space (the Plein) in the center of The Hague.

When walking there, try to imagine the high hedges, vegetable beds, the glass cloches (laid over the tender vegetables as protection against night frosts), the apples and pears, the peaches trained along the walls, and you can picture the relationship of the flower garden in the Binnenhof and the kitchen garden on the modern Plein.

Between the Binnenhof and the Plein, another member of the family, also called Maurice, built his small palace, the Mauritshuis, which was rebuilt in its original style after a fire in the eighteenth century and is now the Mauritshuis Museum. This Maurice acted as the stadtholder's agent. He had a large garden in between the stadtholder's gardens, in which he collected birds and fine sculpture, and where he built a pavilion for his collection of shells and special stones, and kept many exotic plants. He had brought back these plants from Brazil, where he had for a long time been governor for the Republic of the United Provinces.

These arches of yew, here shown with 'White Triumphator', graced the stadtholder's gardens of Prince Maurice and Prince Frederick Henry.

The gardens of Maurice and Frederick Henry of Orange

In the Netherlands, collecting plants was one of Prince Frederick Henry's favorite hobbies, but the half-brother of this celebrated army commander and luxury-loving prince, Prince Maurice, also enjoyed fine gardens. Maurice's garden was in the inner court of the stadtholder's castle, still well-known as the Binnenhof in The Hague. This garden was something very special. It consisted of an elongated area surrounded by green walks. The space was divided into two halves by a green walk running precisely down the middle, producing two almost equal squares. In the middle of these two open spaces was a fountain surrounded by flower beds in which there would undoubtedly have been tulips, widely spaced out.

Above: *Tulipa bakeri* **'Lilac Wonder'.**

Below: 'purissima'.

There was also a two-storied pavilion entirely overgrown with beech hedges. Windows cut in the hedges provided a view from the upper floor over the splendid garden with its geometrical divisions.

The second of the Prince's palaces to survive was once called the Oude Hof (Old Court) and is now known as the Noordeinde Palace. It lies on the Noordeinde, a prominent and distinguished shopping street in The Hague. Frederick Henry was the son of William the Silent and his fourth wife, Louise de Coligny, a French princess. William had bought the Oude Hof for her, had his favorite architect Pieter Post produce a design for its re-building and redecoration, and laid out a fine garden with an island – the Isolotto – in the middle of a lake.

There was also the "Princess's garden," full of flowers, among which, of course, was the tulip, then highly valued as the queen of spring flowers.

Only a few flowers but plenty of atmosphere in this arrangement of 'Orange Favorite', which displays the features of the true Parrot tulip.

A study of the sixteenth- and seventeenth-century collection of tulips in the Hortus Bulborum can give an impression of the varieties of tulips there would have been. The 'Duc van Tol' varieties in particular might have been what Louise de Coligny would have seen in her sheltered and enclosed Princess's garden. These short-stalked tulips resemble the low-growing wild tulips Clusius had acquired from Turkey. In fact, they may well have been bulbs discovered by the great botanist himself.

After the introduction of tulips, bulb growers were quick to work on enlarging the range, so that considerable variation was very soon available. Since tulips were expensive, there were never many on

display, and stocks consisted of a few flowers, which were planted widely apart.

The "Hof te Rijswijck" and the "Huys te Honselaersdijk"

The official stadtholder's residence in The Hague was not a favorite of the prince, who enjoyed hunting and outdoor pursuits. He loved his campaigns in command of his armies, enjoyed lengthy hunting parties, and sought for increased variety and privacy in his private life. His wife, Amalia of Solms, was equally interested in gardens, hunting, and grand houses. They therefore had two enormous hunting lodges – often called pleasances – built, with extensive gardens. The geometrically laid out gardens were filled with statues, fountains, low bushy fruit trees, hedges, walls, and waterways. At the Huys te Honselaersdijk, the great ornamental garden

'Orange Favorite' exudes the elegance of the seventeenth century, an age when profuse arrangements of roses and peonies, fruits, and decorative sea shells were also popular.

was based on circular shapes. At the Hof te Rijswijck, the dominant shapes in the garden were rectangles. Frederick Henry had two gardens to the left and right of his pleasance in Honselaersdijk designed by Louis XIII's famous royal gardener, André Mollet. One was laid out to represent a lion, the other was divided into graceful patterns. Both were adorned with lawns and marble sculpture, and accentuated by box hedges. André Mollet was responsible for many of Louis XIII's gardens.

Besides plants in the open, Frederick Henry also had a large collection of ornamental potted plants.

It was then the custom to have pictures made of the plants in private collections, as was in fact done with

Muscari (grape hyacinths) make a background for
the equally early double tulip 'Marquette'.

the collection at Honselaersdijk. This pictorial
record has provided information on the plants that
were then in this garden, and were already being
imported from abroad, though we do not know
exactly how that was arranged and who was
responsible for it.

Many owners of private gardens, including Caspar
Fagel, Frederick Henry's grand pensionary (one of
his chief advisers), owned enormous collections of
exotic plants, often including many tulips. Both Caspar
Fagel's and Frederick Henry's collections, containing
large numbers of tulip bulbs, were later taken to
Hampton Court by William III when he and his wife
Mary became king and queen of England. Mary in
particular continued to collect exotic plants there,
and built up a magnificent and renowned collection.

One of the successful Triumph tulips is 'Valentine'. This
tulip, 20 in (50 cm) tall, is violet in color. The petals, pale
at the top, are deeper in color nearer the base.

Seventeenth-century English gardens

One of the first garden books to be published in England was *Paradisus*, written by the botanist John Parkinson. It appeared in 1692 and covered more than 140 varieties of plants. Richard Hakluyt had already recorded in 1582 that many kinds of flowers, *Tulipae*, were imported from Austria; possibly, indeed, they were from the Vienna physic garden. The gardens, which included tulips, were laid out in the English version of the renaissance style. Charles I and his wife, Henrietta Maria, sister of the French king Louis XIII, played an important role. They had beautiful gardens at Hampton Court and owned Wimbledon House, which had fine renaissance gardens, designed and planted with the help of André Mollet, the architect of the French royal gardens. Beside the grassy lawns were flowers in beds and in borders. The extremely costly tulips, the novelty of the day, were a sign of power and respect, even if the display was a modest one. Tulips were too expensive for even royalty to be able to have quantities of them.

Many aristocratic garden lovers in seventeenth-century England were deeply interested in the formal style of their gardens. Roy Strong's magnificent book, *The English Renaissance Garden*, gives an excellent account of them. Unfortunately, few of these renaissance gardens have survived.

'Yellow purissima' is a form of *Tulipa fosteriana* here shown forming a graceful curve.

Perhaps the best known is Levens Hall in Cumbria, in the north-west of England. Miraculously, the old pattern dating from between 1689 and 1712 has been preserved next to the Scottish renaissance-style castle. Straight paths, square and rectangular beds are all enclosed with box hedges. The once small clipped yews, set out in the seventeenth century, have now grown into world-famous examples of the art of topiary.

The slave responsible for clipping garden hedges in the Roman empire was called a *topiarius*. Might the word topiary be a relic of the more than two centuries during which Britain under Roman rule became familiar with new forms of gardening?

The clipped shapes at Levens Hall divert the attention from the beds once filled with exotic low-growing plants. There would have been various kinds of flowers, including white lilies, tulips, hyacinths, and daffodils.

Interestingly, the garden lacks a central feature and is simply made up of rectangular areas. Nor is there any important feature closing it off, but just a wall against which peaches, and perhaps figs, were once trained. Cumbria enjoys a warm Gulf Stream climate, which allows such southern plants to survive.

A renaissance garden in Cornwall

One of the most remarkable castellated country houses in Cornwall is Lanhydrock. It is a gray building built around a U-shaped court.

In front, at the opening of the U, is a wide terraced

'Maureen' has long oval flowers and is about 20 in (50 cm) high.

lawn; its sides are at a higher level. A steep grass bank joins the lower to the higher level. This creates an integrated design both to the left and right of the entrance. It is emphasized by very old conical clipped yews, spaced regularly on the lawn in rows, like sentries, symbolizing the apostles.

Biblical symbolism was popular at the time of Elizabeth I, and there are other examples in English gardens, with twelve yew trees planted in a single row, or in two rows of six opposite each other.

In Packwood House, Warwickshire, and at Darthington Hall, Devon, twelve Irish yews (*Taxus baccata* 'Fastigiata'), stand along one side of a long path, with a glorious border of herbs planted along the other side. Oddly enough there, too, are terraced lawns are arranged in the form of an enormous open-air theater.

A small hill sometimes symbolizes the holy hill of Golgotha, as in Packwood House. Such hills are called mounds, and there is more than one explanation for such mounds in a garden or courtyard. The most important is that they gave a good view over the country, so that in the event of a siege or hostile raid all the enemy's movements could be closely observed.

During the Renaissance it was common to lay out what were called "knot gardens." These were gardens with complicated patterns of hedges. The hedges were narrow and low, but twisted around each other in geometrical shapes. Many of these patterns have been preserved and can still be seen in a number of gardens.

Above: 'White Triumphator'.

In Stratford-upon-Avon, next to Shakespeare's house, contemporary with Elizabeth I, is a reconstruction of a knot garden, unfortunately not filled with the plants that would have been appropriate to it.

A more recent example of a knot garden is found near the garden of Barnsley House, Gloucestershire, laid out by Rosemary Verey. She has used a mixture of various hedge plants, green and silver-edged box, and *Teucrium chamaedrys*. At Lanhydrock there are also attractive patterns for a large parterre garden filled with flowers.

In Elizabethan times, many exotic plants were discovered in other continents, which had until then held no interest for Englishmen in this field. For instance, in Virginia, John Tradescant found the first specimens of many wild plants which he took back to England with him. *Tradescantia*, also sometimes called Moses-in-the-cradle, is named after him.

People wanted to be able to have a good look at these exciting new plants, so that special, somewhat narrower and smaller beds were designed to hold a single plant each.

In Lanhydrock all these ideas – the flat open garden, the division of the space into sections, and the knot garden – have been combined in a single colorful flower garden. In the early spring tulips bloom there in multicolored profusion. In this case the abundance of color is appropriate, and an example of a time when polychromatic clashes of color in gardens were not regarded as ugly or uncivilized.

Anyone interested in Elizabeth's choice of flowers should take a look at the portraits of the red-headed queen. Her low-cut dresses had magnificent lace collars, and the material of her gowns was decorated or embroidered with her favorite flowers: many varieties of carnations, daisies, roses symbolic of love, fleur-de-lys as the symbol of royalty, and white lilies symbolic of her inviolable royal status.

A German flower painter

Maria Sybilla Merian was an interesting and talented flower painter. Her father, P. Lauremberg, published *Apparatus Plantorius* in Frankfurt in 1632, with some splendid illustrations of tulips. Some of these tulips grew in the gardens of the Count Von Ruitner, whose estate marched with that of Lauremberg. It is alleged that the talented Maria Sybilla stole some tulips from the count's gardens to paint them for her father's publication.

Later she painted many more tulips, which she admired so much. This was made easier by her move to the Netherlands, where she joined a strict religious sect, the Labadists, who were particularly strong in Friesland. She later went to hunt for exotic flowers in South America, where she painted flowers that had been completely unknown until then. She

This red Parrot tulip is appropriately called 'Red Parrot'.

White tulips go well with white narcissi, anemones, and hyacinths, and with mulberry, cherry, and pear blossom.

specialized in painting animals and shells along with flowers, so that her flower paintings were more than purely botanical prints. She was particularly good at painting butterflies. Tulips were popular in the brilliant gardens the numerous German princes had laid out round their residences. They bloomed in the garden of the Zwinger palace in Dresden, in the Berlin Lustgarten, and many other places.

The design of renaissance gardens remained strictly symmetrical and geometric. Some German gardens were laid out on an enormous scale, such as the Herrenhausen garden in Hanover in 1690, and were furnished extensively with statues, grottoes, and pavilions.

Below: This lily-flowered tulip, called 'Jacqueline', is superbly displayed in a well-designed garden.

Above: 'Sweetheart'.

The decline of the tulip

No flower has been the cause of so much excitement as the tulip. The scarcity in supply, particularly of striped tulips, made prices rise, skillfully encouraged by the bulb owners who were anxious to keep their stocks to themselves, or to get the highest possible price for them. However, there were also pure speculators, who hoped to be able to sell dearly bought tulip bulbs for even more money. Selling prices of tulips were in those days quoted by the aas, approximately 1/32nd of a pennyweight, or 1/200th of a gram; the weight of bulbs in the ground was estimated by this measure and the price determined accordingly. Great fortunes could be made as a bulb was sold on from one buyer to another, with the price rising each time as successive middle men took their profit. It was possible to "earn" huge sums of

Above left: A special tulip from the Hortus Bulborum in Limmen, the Netherlands.

Above right: A bright red, very fine *fosteriana* tulip is 'Galata', one of the rather taller varieties of this species.

Below right: Single early tulips make up a large group. Here is *Tulipa* 'Sint Maarten' which flowers in March.

money in the tulip trade. It is clear from the Dutch government's efforts to regulate the trade that many people were worried by these steeply rising prices. Their attempts at regulation were in vain. The dealers met in small hostelries or in the fields to sell their wares, disregarding any regulations. Sometimes complete inheritances were squandered, with horses, cattle, furniture, and whole harvests being staked in order to gain possession of a few tulips to sell on.

On February 3, 1637, this trade, usually referred to as "tulipomania," went wrong. Some dealers had met in a small inn and were playing a dangerous game in their Dutch auction.

Offers were made for a pound weight of tulips. At once someone bid 1,250 florins. No one had confidence in this bid, and the game was repeated with the next lot of tulip bulbs, which now went for 150 florins less than the previous lot of the same weight. The game was repeated a third time, and the price fell again. It became obvious that the real value of the bulbs was no longer at issue, but that prices had been driven up so steeply that they no longer had any relation to real values. The news that something had gone wrong spread rapidly. Tulip dealers wanted to prevent a catastrophe and clearly wanted to make agreements among themselves to fix prices for the bulbs.

A meeting in Utrecht attracted great interest, with delegates representing all the large trading towns of the time. However, a decision could not be reached and prices again became the sport of the highest bidder. Tulips were able to command high prices once more, but many investors were ruined later in the same year. Prices fell dramatically. Anyone who had not sold in time made a loss. Many finished up poorer than when they had begun, though those with a little more sense had taken appropriate action at the right moment.

What must a man like Adriaan Pauw, lord of Heemstede, Bennebroek and Nieuwerkerk, have

Above: This is the *fosteriana* tulip 'Robassa'.

thought when he looked at his tulips, planted all around a mirrored gazebo, an octagonal pavilion? In 1636, a year before the market for tulips had crashed, he had been offered 12,000 florins for ten bulbs of *Tulipa semper Augustus*. Adriaan Pauw had, however, refused to sell his bulbs for that or any other price, and he was the man who held the exchequer, and was in fact treasurer of the provinces of Holland and West-Friesland. It must have been a bitter pill to swallow, to look at tulips that had once been so valuable and know that they no longer represented real money. Clearly after 1637 people saw tulips in a different light. And yet *Tulipa* was still worth something. Moreover, one significant advantage emerged from the disaster: in their search for the best methods of cultivation, the growers had acquired a great deal of know-how in the production and storage of the various types of bulbs. Dutch tulip

Tulipa **'Salmon Parrot' is a Parrot tulip. For 300 years it has been known that it cannot be propagated from seed. It makes a delightful challenge for flower arrangers.**

traders really knew their bulbs, and this enabled them to maintain their unique position for centuries to come. There was competition from growers in Belgium and particularly from Valenciennes in France, where tulips were also grown. With imports from Holland and West-Friesland they supplied the growing demand created by seventeenth- and early eighteenth-century tulip lovers. Each year enormous quantities of tulips were grown for the royal gardens and to complement ladies' dresses. They were also grown in the Netherlands to provide cut flowers, nosegays, and bouquets.

CHAPTER 7

Gardens in the Time of William and Mary

Whereas Louis XIV could make use
of talented architects like Le
Veaux, decorators like Le Brun, and
landscape architects like Le Nôtre, such
experts were still in short supply at the time
of William and Mary. Louis XIV had built
the brilliant palace of Versailles, which was
to be the model for so many elsewhere. It was
famous for its enormous extent, and for the
size, wealth, and elegant decoration –
unprecedented at that time – of its salons and
gardens. This was only made possible by the
large numbers of highly trained craftsmen
employed in France on the creation of
buildings, interiors, and gardens. Hence
France set the tone, and French craftsmen
traveled to Russia, England, the
Netherlands, Spain, and Austria. These
craftsmen were also popular in Germany. So
it is not surprising that William III, who in
his youth had had to put up with living in
reduced circumstances, after his first
successes as stadtholder and as a military
commander, wished to taste the pleasure of
creating a magnificent environment.

**Just as in the sixteenth century, Clusius's time, geometric
shapes are still used for tulip beds.**

In this he took the advice of the best Dutch artists and architects and also attracted craftsmen living outside the Netherlands. His palace at Het Loo was designed in all secrecy by architects of the Royal Academy of Architecture in Paris. The Dutch ambassador asked this academy to design a hunting lodge for a wealthy, important private individual in the Low Countries. This was done, and the design, which would later turn out to be the design for the hunting lodge of Het Loo, was taken to the Netherlands. There it was adapted, perhaps with a few alterations, by Jacob Roman, who was William and Mary's royal architect.

Daniel Marot, a decorator, engraver, and architect trained entirely in France, also influenced the processing of the French designs, and was particularly involved with the interior decoration and the gardens; for these he worked in collaboration with Jacob Roman. At that time, it was common practice for the architect to design the gardens.

Tulips were an important feature in the gardens laid out for William and Mary, who was a great connoisseur of flowering and orangery plants. Particular attention was devoted to tulips, not only in the gardens, but in interior decoration too, with special vases for them in the private apartments. These still famous Delft blue vases are known as tulip vases.

Formal influences are to be found not only in the gardens of castles and country houses. Round, oval, and lozenge shapes are also used for special flower beds near farmhouses, such as this one in the Netherlands.

Tulip vases in Het Loo

Visitors to Het Loo Palace can see the tulip vases used in Mary's time. One of these antique vases, painted with blue tulips, stands in her sitting room, which looks out over the large garden. The decoration shows up beautifully on the white porcelain that Delft was so skilled at producing. The tulips could be arranged in individual little spouts or openings in the vases to give the impression of a pyramid of flowers.

Unlike other flowers, such as lilies, tulips have relatively short stalks, restricting the opportunities for their arrangement. Certainly small, tight little bouquets were not appropriate for the high rooms of seventeenth-century houses, so these special vases were invented to show the allure and value of tulips to their best advantage. The potter made the vase in sections, so that there were various levels which could hold water. Even the top sections of these tall tulip vases contained water for the tulips, which draped themselves gracefully from the openings. Because a tulip in a vase tends to turn upwards, their sometimes almost horizontal, and sometimes more vertical position, gave these arrangements an impression of reaching for unseen heights. Such vases were made in various shapes, sometimes small and sometimes 28–32 in (70–80 cm.) high or more. They were very costly, as was all Delft

Marcel Wolterinck created this arrangement for an iron renaissance vase. Real tulip vases consist of a set of vases of decreasing size standing one on the other, with the smallest at the top.

porcelain, but in this case the additional crafts-manship involved in the elegant and difficult to apply painting made them even more so.

William and Mary owned a number of these vases, which were favorite objects for collection through-out Europe. One of the largest is in Chatsworth, in Derbyshire, where today it is unfortunately filled with artificial tulips. These vases are being made again in Portugal and Spain fashioned in earthen-ware in the style of old models. Modern artists and potters like Jan van der Vaart have applied themselves to this art and have created really fine modern variants of seventeenth-century tulip vases.

Tulips were often painted arranged in bouquets. It is remarkable that in these pictures they are always shown tall, as if they had long stalks. They were also painted on Dresden porcelain, produced and decorated in the famous Meissen factory.

Antique statues have been endlessly copied, and century after century new ways of arranging them have been found. Here tulips ('Dreamland') are used as a decoration beside a garden seat and a concrete goddess on a pedestal.

Striped tulips appear on French porcelain from Sèvres, too. They provide a fine show on Delft and Loosdrecht porcelain from the Netherlands as well. The popular striped tulips are repeatedly depicted on plates, vases, and dishes.

Tulips in paintings – the "cartoons"

Flower painters have almost always felt themselves free to place flowers in their arrangements wherever it suited them best. In one of the works of Pieter Breughel, who painted magnificent flower pieces, there is an enormous bouquet, standing much taller

Above: Lily-shaped petals are popular in 'Triumphator' tulips.

Below: Tulips accentuate the color of the garden seat and the house.

than its stalks could ever have made possible. Such meticulous brushwork could never have been achieved in the time available. The flowers would have wilted and would certainly no longer be in full bloom in the garden before the painting was finished. So a little trick was employed. The flowers were painted in full bloom on a piece of cheap card, or sometimes on canvas. They were painted from the front, from behind, from the sides, from above, and from below; the paintings were kept as reference material. When a flower painting was wanted, the artist worked from these "cartoons," sometimes for a specific commission, sometimes when the studio had nothing else to do. Students had to learn their trade from a master who could to a large extent leave them to make these paintings for him, though he then painted the difficult parts himself. With this method of painting flower pieces, the flowers could be arranged in any way the artist liked.

Placing tulips centrally or in a dominating position in an arrangement increases their interest and importance. The beautiful shape of the tulip and its stalk makes the flower particularly suitable to give a free and graceful character to such a painting. Tulips are therefore often portrayed at the sides or bending forwards, and are nearly always the most prominent feature in such paintings.

Paintings of flowers, and particularly of striped tulips, were popular from a very early date. A great diversity is to be found in many museums and private collections, and they demonstrate vividly why striped tulips were once valued so highly. Only much later do the painted bouquets show the

originally less highly valued, plain shapes of uniformly colored tulips. This tells us exactly at which point they, too, began to be treasured.

Tulips in William and Mary's gardens

In 1689 the Dutch prince and English princess were crowned king and queen of England. For Mary this was a logical step.

In her opinion and in that of the English Protestants, the Anglicans, her father James II was too Catholic, and encouraged the Roman faith too strongly. The king was forced to flee to Catholic France. William's mother, another Mary Stuart, was also the daughter

A host of "chattering" Parrot tulips sway in sun and wind: 'Flaming Parrot'.

of a king of England, and sister of James II and his brother and predecessor, Charles II.

Family connections were therefore sufficient to justify William's claim to the throne, and allowed him eventually to become king. Yet the Dutch prince was not crowned with the wholehearted agreement of all the English. It was in fact Mary's refusal to bear the responsibility alone which was the deciding factor. Accordingly his political opponents changed tack and accepted a Dutch king.

Immediately after 1688, William's efforts in England were entirely engaged in leading the army he had ferried across from Holland. After several attempts to cross in rough weather, which resulted in hundreds of horses being drowned and substantial damage to his ships, he succeeded in landing in stormy weather at Torbay, in the south of England.

His father-in-law, James, set out from London with the English army to meet him. However, it never came to a battle. James fell ill, returned to London, and from there fled under cover of night, first by coach and then by ship, to France.

The coronation took place a year later, and Mary came over from the Netherlands, where she had been able to indulge her passion for flowers, gardens, and houses. She left a whole range of palaces and hunting lodges behind her: Huis te Rijswijck, Hof te Honselaersdijk, Noordeinde Palace, Huis ten Bosch, and Soestdijk Palace, quite apart from the royal hunting lodges of Dieren and Het Loo.

Airy formality is always popular, as witness this rose arbor, clipped hedges, and tulips with their shrouded shades: Parrot tulip 'Black Parrot'.

Above: 'Madame Lefebre' in the Hortus Bulborum, Limmen.

Below: 'Galata' is an antique tulip with a pointed flower head.

These houses often had spacious gardens with large orangeries and many pot plants, and hundreds of gardeners were employed on their upkeep. Tulips were planted in all of them in large quantities, but always wide apart. They were set around the lawns in special flower borders. Box hedges and gravel filled the spaces not covered by lawns or flowers.

There were various designs and divisions, and many different kinds of parterre. A familiar one is the *parterre de broderie*, where a border was planted with flowers around the central area of grass and gravel. In the spring tulips, daffodils, and hyacinths were followed by lilies, perennials, and annuals as colorful accents, all planted at a distance from each other. In between, yews and junipers clipped into points provided vertical elements. Rambling roses, too, were trained along standards to give vertical accents. These gardens were full of statuary, fountains, and vases, some of them with a display of tulips. A visit to the seventeenth-century gardens of the Het Loo Palace offers a perfect example of such a garden.

Dutch garden ideas in England

Mary's hundreds of varieties of rock plants were supplemented by William's many purchases. He acquired special collections from various garden owners in the Netherlands.

Moreover, many exotic plants were brought from all

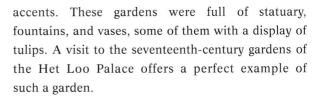

A spring flower arrangement in a green iron vase has some Parrot tulips lying beside it, ready to be handed to visitors.

Above: Oriental colors will suit an exotic bouquet.

Below: Green tulips make a good combination with *Helleborus corsicus* and *H. foetidus*.

parts of the world by the ships of the East and West India Companies at the special request of the royal couple. As a result Mary's collection was one of the most complete then in existence. Sadly she did not return to the Netherlands, and never saw her gardens again, or the final enhancement of Het Loo with its greatly extended grounds.

However, she could give full rein to her hobby in England, first at Kensington Palace, and later in the enormous gardens at Hampton Court. Mary concentrated on the pots and the rare plants, while William had more of an eye for the whole ensemble. Not only the gardens of Kensington Palace attracted attention, but particularly those at Hampton Court where alterations were undertaken. William had a *parterre de broderie* laid out to a design by the French Huguenot Daniel Marot in the semi-circular

space between the new façade of his enlarged palace and the Grand Canal. The Grand Canal itself had been constructed by Charles II. Small pointed yews were planted there and are now the only survivors of this seventeenth-century planting.

The yews are now monuments in themselves, having grown completely out of proportion into fantastic but far too large trees.

Several small gardens between the River Thames and the palace have also survived from William and Mary's time. They are small, well-shaped, sunken flower gardens. Unfortunately there is little understanding

This is how the tulip was displayed in sixteenth- and seventeen-century gardens: single flowers which could be admired from all sides. Its isolation emphasized the value of each tulip.

This sparkling tulip is 'Keizerskroon'; arranged in a basket it would make a fine Easter display.

of historical planting schemes at Hampton Court, and there are now totally inappropriate annuals in the flower beds. There should be seventeenth- and early eighteenth-century tulips, since extensive lists of the right varieties exist. The Hortus Bulborum in Limmen could supply the right plants, together with seventeenth-century daffodils, hyacinths, and crown imperial varieties, so that a real "William and Mary garden" could be re-created.

The baroque gardens of Het Loo Palace

One of the most spectacular reconstructions of seventeenth-century gardens is in the Netherlands: the baroque garden of Het Loo, the palace of the

House of Orange, which has been returned completely to its seventeenth-century state. The word Loo means "a place where many streams flow," and that was in fact the reason for William and Mary's choice of this spot to build a hunting lodge. While it was being built, they lived in the medieval castle Het Oude Loo, which is still preserved in its original form. In building the house for their hunting lodge, no expense or effort was spared to produce something of remarkable beauty, both in the garden and in the interior decoration. Inside the house, the walls were covered with mural paintings, while outside vases, statues, freestone cascades, and long basins with fountains were laid out. And all this in the grandiose manner ascribed both to the architect of the house, Jacob Roman, and the designer of the flowering parterres, Daniel Marot. The garden was excavated to a level several yards (meters) below that

Above: Put pale-colored tulips in dark places.

Below: *Tulipa* **'Gentile' in the Botanic Garden at Haren.**

of the house, so that the design of the parterres would show up well from it. In the center was a statue of Venus with Tritons, demi-gods spouting water, around her feet, and there were also statues in the larger parterres. In the lower garden, at each end of the cross axis running at right angles to the main broad walk, there were two large globes on pedestals. One depicted the four continents throughout which the East India Company was already trading; stone figures and beasts represented the continents. The other showed the sky, or more accurately, the firmament of heaven. Jets of water erupted from the signs of the Zodiac on the celestial globe, which also indicates Mary's date of birth, a demonstration of how much the garden was designed for its owners. On the left of the house was William's garden, another parterre, with orange and blue flowers in

A mixed bouquet full of atmosphere.

summer, and a sunken lawn – a bowling green. This was also used for a variant of croquet popular at the time.

To the right of the house was Mary's garden. Part was laid out as parterres with many flower borders and plenty of space for her collection of exotic plants in pots and tubs. Another section was reserved for an extensive arbor walk. Half of this covered walk has been reconstructed and shows how unbelievably magical and impressive it must have been at its full original length.

Tulips in the garden of Het Loo

In reconstructing this garden, which was filled in with earth in the nineteenth century, the object was to keep as far as possible to the seventeenth-century planting scheme, in order to show a complete image of a single period. This included roses, hellebores, standard roses, nasturtiums, marigolds, and many other types of plants then common in gardens. That was the whole point: to get the selection which was actually used in the seventeenth century.

This went for the tulips, too, which were supplied by the Hortus Bulborum in Limmen. Their selection of historical tulips is unequaled in the world today. Every year new bulbs are produced, so that visitors interested in the history of the tulip can see the seventeenth-century varieties, set wide apart in the ornamental beds. At that time people were anxious to have a good look at the enormously expensive tulips, and arranged their display so that each plant could be admired separately as if it were a valuable gem.

With their beautiful color and shape many tulips can be used both for planting in the garden and for arrangements.

Display cabinets

Private individuals as well as universities started making plant collections. The Orange family, the stadtholders, who had helped to free the Low Countries from Spanish rule, played a leading role in starting the fashion. William I of Orange, called "the Silent," was too busily engaged with his political innovations and his war against Spain, which, together with the demands of his four successive wives, took up too much of his time for him to be able to create a special garden at the Prinsenhof where he lived in Delft.

His sons did better. Prince Maurice is known to have had a splendid garden laid out in the Binnenhof in The Hague, the current center of government, at that time his stadtholder's castle in the center of the modern city.

Below left: 'Page Polka' is the cheerful name of this Triumph tulip.

Maurice's brother, Prince Frederick Henry, was a born collector. He lived at a time when people collected not only plants, but also animals, special stones, skeletons, dried plants, and shells. Ships returning from South Africa, Asia, Indonesia, America, Canada, and South America, brought these objects home on their trading trips. They were seen as curiosities for which there was often a special demand from rich collectors. Sailors were frequently commissioned to look out for these objects, and the collections were displayed to visitors in special cabinets.

Above: 'Green Spot' (a greenish-white *viridiflora* tulip), and 'Fantasy' (a pink Parrot tulip).

Left: The desire to collect a wide variety of tulips has not been lost. Because the tulips planted here are in narrow inter-woven strips, this garden resembles the weave of a Persian carpet, which often had patterns inspired by flowers.

The garden as a display cabinet

Apart from these collections, set out in display cabinets specially constructed to show them off, there were also plant collections. Plants were collected to satisfy a personal interest, but also to impress family, friends, and business acquaintances. They lent increased respect and gave an impression of scholarship, which pleased many collectors. And so tulips were collected and displayed in spaciously laid out gardens.

Gardens elsewhere in Europe

Gardens in France

As early as the sixteenth century there were various French gardens worth looking at. The interest in tulips which arose during the reign of Louis XIV, was evident in the gardens at his court, and in the gardens of nobles, rich bankers, and merchants was also expressed in decoration and in dress. Louis XIV's mistress, Madame de Pompadour, who was endowed with intelligence as well as beauty, led the fashion, which was promptly followed by all affluent ladies. She created beautiful sprays to wear on her shoulder and in her hair, using not only tulips, but also lilies of the valley, lavender, roses, and even sprigs of lilac.

The sanitary provisions of the time offered no oppor-tunity for a daily bath to the finely dressed ladies and gentlemen. They washed their faces a little, their hands and wrists, and perhaps occasionally their whole body, though that was considered extremely risky. Undoubtedly scented flowers were chosen for that reason. To make the purpose of the scent less obvious, beautiful flowers were chosen for sprays to wear on dresses. Tulips were among them when they were in flower, and were exceptionally popular. Flowers from the surroundings of Lisse and Haarlem were transported to Versailles and the Louvre. How that was done is a marvel. The tulips were picked green and taken to the court by fast mail coach.

A mouthwatering sight for flower arrangers: 'Shirley' single late tulips, which bend their tall stems gracefully in a rush basket or a glass vase.

The tulip was pre-eminently considered to be a special royal flower, which, quite independently of the Dutch tulipomania, was gaining increasing popularity in many countries of Europe. Not only the gardens of Versailles and of the Louvre, the royal palace in Paris, but also the St Cloud palace of the Duke of Orléans, the King's brother, were famous for their tulip gardens. Louis XV's son was the art-loving Louis XVI. His wife, the beautiful daughter of the empress Maria Theresa, was Marie Antoinette. Her great interest in the idea of turning back to nature to find the truth, the essence of existence, led her to make changes in a corner of the enormous gardens at Versailles. She had a "hamlet" built, a group of buildings based on a Norman farmhouse, or at least looking a little like one, which was a pleasant oasis for the queen where she could enjoy watching her lambs, goats, ducks, and pigeons. There was a small meadow with a stream and a lake, and everything radiated happiness and simplicity. In these surroundings, she delighted in wearing simple loose-fitting dresses tied with ribbons around the waist or under the bust. Beautiful paintings have survived of this lovely queen in the light clothing she wore in her "hamlet." Flowers were her second great love, and among them were tulips in all their varieties and in great quantities. They were used in the garden for flower borders and for bouquets.

Gardens in Germany

Tulips were collected in Germany, too; and even in far-away Brazil they were planted by the empress

A "royal" tulip, 'Scarlet King', in the Hortus Bulborum.

Leopoldine, who came from Europe, in the garden of her palace in Petropolis.

In Germany tulips can be found in the magnificent Nymphenburg garden at Schloss Mirabell in Salzburg, and also in the gigantic garden of Herrenhausen in Hanover, where the Electress Sophia had an enormous garden laid out around her grand palace. Dutch gardeners and architects produced the design, and helped to implement it. This enormous baroque garden had great *parterres de broderie*. Tulips were planted in the flower borders around the lawns, the areas of marble chippings, and box hedges. There was still more to admire. There were splendid pools, tall hedges dividing the gardens into "rooms", and lanes of clipped trees. There was also a theatre with gilded statues, such as the one in St. Petersburg in Russia.

Above: The striking, intensely red *Tulipa praestans* 'Fusilier'.

Below: 'Salmon Parrot', a Parrot tulip.

The whole estate was one of the special sights in the west of Germany. Elsewhere, too, in Prussia, fine gardens were laid out by Dutch garden designers or architects.

The palaces of that period in Oranienberg and Oranienstein have survived. They yearn for the restoration of their seventeenth-century gardens, and for the tulips, which used to be planted there in large quantities.

Just as in Brandenburg, the daughters of Prince Frederick Henry took Dutch garden culture with them to Germany, and made flower gardens popular there, too.

Peter the Great in Russia

Another ruler interested in tulips was Peter the Great. This Russian tsar spent a long time in western

Above: The Parrot tulip 'Blue Parrot' is also suitable for special arrangements.

Europe, and traveled widely, particularly in Holland. He was a great admirer of William III, and studied shipbuilding, architecture, garden design, and horticulture in the Netherlands. He had a large garden laid out around the palace he built in St. Petersburg.

The design was by French architects. In this he followed the example of William III, who too made use of the expertise of the Royal Academy of Architecture in Paris for the design of Het Loo palace. Peter the Great also visited Versailles, where he was very impressed with the gardens.

The St. Petersburg gardens are mainly architectural, divided by gilded statues, cascades, water channels, and other dramatic effects. They are not designed for small flowers.

William and Mary's interest in tulips was enough incentive for Peter the Great, too, to plant them in his gardens. That the St. Petersburg Botanic Gardens later played an important role in the discovery of wild varieties of tulip is a consequence of the tradition of collecting plants and considering them of sufficient importance to establish a special garden for them, where they could be carefully tended.

'Duc van Tol Roze' in the foreground in the Hortus Bulborum at Limmen.

CHAPTER 8

Gardens in the 17th- and 18th-Century Williamsburg

The Governor's House in Williamsburg

Near Richmond, the capital of the American state of Virginia, is William and Mary College. This famous college, founded on the initiative of the king and queen of England whose names it bears, is still flourishing, and has preserved its buildings in very good condition.

The handsome brick architecture is distinguished, warm in color, and clear in design. On the right, as you enter the College, is the lecture theater with wooden benches. At the back, in wings built out to left and right, are the refectory and the assembly hall. Above are more teaching rooms and the professors' quarters. The whole atmosphere is one of dignified tranquility without frills.

In the old state capital, beautifully restored and in part reconstructed, which was named Williamsburg after William, the integral town plan has been preserved. A high street is planted with centuries-old trees, and at the end of it is the College, opposite the Court House Justitie.

This violet-pink Triumph tulip is called 'Rosario'. Here it is arranged in a fine bunch.

Unfortunately the original Governor's House, the home of the state governor of Virginia, burned down, but substantial contributions from the Rockefeller family have made it possible to reconstruct what had been lost, covering the three hundred years of the town's existence. What was left of the old houses and public buildings was also restored, as well as the Governor's House, which is a shining example of the classic Dutch seventeenth- and eighteenth-century style. The garden was reconstructed with the help of the Historic Garden Society of Virginia, which has re-established many gardens with excellent taste, restraint, and a feel for austerity. The garden behind Governor's House is divided into a number of sections. Immediately behind the building are diamond-shaped beds surrounded with box, and filled with tulips in spring and annuals in summer. Behind,

at a lower level, is a lawn, a long straight stretch leading to a handsome iron gate. To the left and right are ancient trees. Below them, long beds are filled with tulips in spring. The whole scene would give an authentic impression, if only the varieties of tulips were not too modern. However, the organizers may be forgiven, as such large quantities would be required that they could probably not find enough seventeenth-century tulip bulbs anywhere. Now red and white Darwin tulips stand there with their tall straight stems. There is an ornamental flower garden, too, as well as a fruit garden and a box garden.

The need to protect flowers and vegetables from predators was the original reason for hedges, screens, and walls. Here a gateway of yew leads to white lily-flowered 'White Triumphator' tulips.

The renaissance garden as a model for modern interpretations of gardens

The renaissance garden can still serve as a model for present-day gardens in many ways. First, all the fifteenth-, sixteenth-, and early seventeenth-century gardens preserved in paintings, prints, and designs can be studied whenever a period garden needs to be restored or reconstructed. Second, this type of garden can serve as a source of inspiration whenever a totally new garden has to be laid out in the renaissance style. This happens more often than one might imagine. There are, for instance, surprisingly convincing renaissance gardens in America which, though they were mostly laid out in the seventeenth or early eighteenth centuries, in essence maintain the renaissance model both in design and proportions.

In many places in Virginia you can find reconstructions or interpretations designed by the Garden Club of Virginia. One such magical spot is in Williamsburg, where, though many thousands of people troop through it every year, the refinement and restraint of a private renaissance garden have been retained.

Behind the many wooden houses of the high street, which runs between William and Mary College and the Court House, are found gardens laid out with box hedges, beautiful wooden fences, topiary, brick paths, and flower borders. The beautifully clipped yews and box, and apple, pear, and crab apple

Red strawberries and red 'Rococo' Parrot tulips make up a compact arrangement.

Above: 'Salmon Parrot' glows like a flamingo.

Below: 'Green Spot' and 'Salmon Parrot', a Parrot tulip.

shrubs, provide fascinating accents in the formally laid-out gardens, which taken as a whole are a unique collection of renaissance gardens. It has been possible to reconstruct much in Williamsburg from old drawings which have survived, and the gaps have been filled in with taste and a feeling for style. The great variety of shape and content prevents any suggestion of dullness here.

Tulips in Williamsburg

Herbs were popular in these gardens, as were vegetables, apples, and pears. They were mainly meant to be "utility" gardens, but also had sections planted with ornamental plants, some of which had been brought as seeds and bulbs on the perilous ocean crossing from the Netherlands, England, and all the other European countries from which the immigrants had come.

The centuries-old garden wall of Castle Bingerden, Angerloo, hides many tempting garden secrets. Tulips introduce the apricot-salmon color which is later continued in perennials and roses.

Obviously flowers were not a top priority to take when emigrating. Cattle and household goods were more important for survival in a land inhabited by possibly hostile Natives. That seeds were taken in spite of this shows how precious some of the flowers must have been. It is not surprising that tulips were among them. Together with wild columbines, the red and yellow wild columbine of Virginia, with wild native phlox, daisies, wild hyacinths, daffodils, and scillas, they now bloom in the simple, but just for that reason more convincing, renaissance gardens of Williamsburg, Virginia.

Jefferson's eighteenth-century garden at Monticello

Thomas Jefferson was America's second president. He was a well-read and well-traveled man, who was very interested in the natural sciences. For some years he was the American ambassador to France. This indefatigable fighter against English rule built himself a grand house which he called Monticello. It, too, is situated in the state of Virginia. The house is a completely white building, which could have come straight from the area round Venice. Yet this amateur-architect did not just make a plain copy. Both inside and out, its design and layout are highly original. Jefferson was also an inventor, and the whole house shows interesting evidences of it. Terraces to the left and right of the main house expand its shape to a horse-shoe and lead to the garden. Behind the house is the private flower garden, with a collection of all kinds of rare plants. Rare carnations, irises, roses, and many shrubs and fruit trees were collected by this botanist, and naturally he also planted numerous tulips in his flower garden, importing them from Holland. Unfortunately here, too, modern varieties of tulips have been planted. Today we are blinded by their vivid, bright colors, whereas the short-stemmed seventeenth- and eighteenth-century varieties would be far preferable, but again, the big problem would have been procurement.

Above: In Jefferson's garden at Monticello this antique *Tulipa* 'Gentile' would complement perfectly his collection of shrubs and trees.

Above: *Tulipa* **'Menton' has long stalks, which make it suitable for backgrounds and for tall arrangements.**

Tulipa kaufmanniana **'Stresa' blooms yellow and red.**

During his time in France, he became familiar with neo-classicism, and went on to study the architecture of Palladio, the fifteenth-century Italian architect. He would undoubtedly have studied Palladio's *Quatro Libri dell'architetura* before he started building his own house, Monticello, with its central section and two semi-circular wings strongly inspired by fifteen-and early sixteenth-century Italian architecture. The interior is neo-classical, but with Jefferson's own original emendations; he produced an integrated design of his own house, combining his own interior decoration, his own clock, and many other inventions of his own. The garden consisted of three important sections, which still survive to be admired by anyone visiting the house and gardens, now a national monument. Behind the house is a semi-circular, somewhat elliptical lawn, encircled by a path. Along it are borders planted with favorite shrubs and trees. Sadly, the administrators have not so far been able to obtain a supply of the right eighteenth-century bulbs, though they can be ordered in the Netherlands. They have used modern Darwin tulips, which may be colorful, but are not historically correct. At the front of the house, the garden is laid out as a park with wide lawns, dotted with trees. A driveway follows the line of the semi-circle formed by the main house with its two wings. Everything here is concentrated on the brilliant prospect, which just as in English landscape gardens and parkland is framed by the individually placed trees. The third garden is the kitchen garden, which is at a lower level, parallel to one of the wings. This is an accurate reconstruction, and includes the outbuildings which stood there in Jefferson's time.

CHAPTER 9

Bulb Growing along the North Sea Coast

O*ne of the constraints of tulip growing is the need for a well-drained and fertile soil for the bulbs from the time they are planted out until they are lifted at the end of the summer. There are probably only a few places in the whole world where such soil is to be found, and tulips have established themselves in these places over the centuries. In the Netherlands there is only a limited expanse of such soil. It has been found along the coast between The Hague and Haarlem, and in North Holland near Castricum and Limmen. Clusius would undoubtedly have been pleased that there was such suitable soil so close to Leiden, just behind the dunes, where his bulbs could be grown.*

The marvel of the bulb fields, always laid out in a wide open landscape. The insects which carry viral diseases live in shrubs and bushes: hence bare fields. The multicolored Triumph tulip is called 'Lucky Strike'. For a long time it has been cultivated for the bulbs, and the flowers are picked so as to retain all the vitality in the bulb.

Many other bulb growers who established themselves to the west of Leiden were happy, too. This area became known as "the Dutch bulbfields." At the same time, from the seventeenth century onwards, bulb growers settled to the north of Haarlem, and also further to the north, near Limmen, where the soil was also found to be good. Anyone now visiting the bulbfields around villages such as Sassenheim, Hillegom, and Lisse can see how carelessly the powers that be have treated this historic land. Some is still used for growing tulips, but much is now completely built up with housing and office blocks, an alarming development that needs to be addressed; this region should be made

a conservation area, on which no building should be allowed.

The history of the bulbfields

Be that as it may, this was open ground in the seventeenth century, though quite different in its geographical features. Near Lisse were lakes, of which vestiges still remain, such as the Kagerplassen. There were also lakes which were afterwards made into polders, and drained by windmills. The Haarlemmermeer is a fine example of this. The lakes along the coast had been produced by various causes. Some were relics of river deltas. This is still largely the situation in the western Netherlands. The low-lying areas behind the dunes were dusted with sand, forming good, well-drained soil with a fertile

'Attila' tulips are a bright violet, so that they match the color of ribes, flowering crab apples, and honesty.

substratum of clay. This is what Clusius's bulbs did well on, and the bulbs of the many growers who followed him. The coastal regions at a higher level were some of the earliest inhabited areas of the western part of the Netherlands. The rivers and the sea were navigable, so fishermen settled there. Cattle could be kept on the low-lying fields, and in an emergency taken up to higher land. Apart from farmers and fishermen, it was also inhabited by hunters who could find plenty of deer, hares, pheasants, and wild boar roaming in the areas along the coast.

Towns developed at Leiden, Delft, The Hague, Haarlem, Amsterdam, and Rotterdam. Prince William I, the stadtholder, lived in the Prinsenhof at Delft, now a museum. It was a cultural center where many artists settled. In Leiden there was a famous

university, of which the renowned horticulturalist Clusius was a member from 1592. The Hague became the center of government for the House of Orange, where they were given quarters in the castle, the Binnenhof. Amsterdam became an important port, where ships could lie at anchor in the shelter of the inland sea, the Zuiderzee. It shared its function as a port with Rotterdam, in an ideal situation at the mouth of the River Maas. Antwerp, on the Scheldt estuary in the Southern Netherlands, was a formidable competitor to Rotterdam, and was to remain one for a long time.

These yellow to orange-red double early tulips look well in farms and cottage gardens, but quite obviously the use of these tulips in other kinds of gardens offers many interesting possibilities.

Above: 'Don Quichote'.

Below: Double early tulips grow low.

The Dutch bulbfields were one of the developments between The Hague and Amsterdam. It was also an area where grand country houses were built by rich citizens or noblemen, particularly around The Hague, to be near the Orange court. Amsterdam was a town of citizens, merchants, bankers, and artists. They built their country houses along the River Vecht and near Haarlem. Castles had been built in the past in the region above Haarlem, but few have survived intact. In addition to the advantage of a central position between the large towns, the wild woods on the dunes are a reason for living there. Frederick Henry had special hunting lodges built there, and that he built them to the south of The Hague shows how wooded the area was then. The open land between the spinneys was ideal for hunting foxes, pheasants, rabbits, and hares. So a combination emerged of castles and country houses surrounded by fine gardens, level pastures for cattle, and bulb growing on the sandy soil.

Seventeenth-century methods of cultivation

Early on people realized that they could not grow tulips in the same soil year in and year out. After the harvest, the land had to lie fallow for one or two years, or be planted with some other crop, giving disease germs no opportunity to develop. Preferably, plants were chosen that would add nutrients to the soil for cultivating tulips. The bulbs were planted

Above: Attila forcefully led his Huns, and this tulip named after him vividly symbolizes his character.

'Page Polka' Triumph tulips.

out in September, and as soon as the air began to cool off at night, the planted fields were strewn with straw to prevent the ground freezing. The straw was removed again from the beds in the spring, around March. After the flowers had bloomed, or even while they were still in bloom, the blossoms were broken off the stems to prevent the nutrients from the bulb being used to form seed. The foliage was left unharmed, until it shriveled up naturally and all the nutrients in the leaf had returned to the bulb. A new bulb is formed every year, as soon as the tulip flowers. The flower uses all the nutrition in the bulb. A young bulb develops as soon as the old bulb shrivels up into itself. The leaves and roots provide new nourishment for the new bulb, which goes on developing until it is harvested.

This process was also familiar to the sixteenth- and seventeenth-century bulb growers. They experienced trouble from disease and from mild winters with too much damp and too little frost and snow. They also knew that too much moisture harmed bulbs, a fact that determined the choice of well-drained, sandy soil for the bulbfields. To plant the bulbs, they used a large wooden roller, with laths fixed around the edges. The roller was rolled over the bed to be planted, and the bulbs were planted by means of a small pointed stick, rather thicker at the top. This planting stick made a hole into which the bulb could be dropped with its point upwards.

This simple method enabled the rows of tulips to be planted at the right distance apart in the beds.

CHAPTER 10

France at the End of the 18th Century

The rising in 1789 of "les citoyens de Paris", with the storming of the Bastille, the Paris fortress prison, was the start of the great revolution, and had widespread consequences for the feudal system and for society in large parts of Europe, particularly western Europe. The nobility, widely established since time immemorial, were no longer automatically the rulers. After this social upheaval the citizens, "les citoyens", took over power. At least, that was what they fought for. But a system of pure democracy works almost nowhere, since people always need a leader, even rebels, terrorists, and anarchists. Everyone who has studied world history knows that leadership carries within itself the seeds of corruption. Many intrinsically idealistic movements have eventually ended up as dictatorships.

Under the two *Chamaecyparis* trees are single late tulips 'Maureen' and 'Mrs J.T. Scheepers', which will soon be followed by azaleas, flowering in lemon yellow ('Harvest Moon') and white ('Persil').

'Mrs J.T. Scheepers' in a yellow and white water garden.

This, too, happened during the revolution in France, which was welcomed by many citizens of western Europe. In the Netherlands the situation was less inflammable. Townsfolk, farmers, and other country people had for centuries exercised power there.

The Netherlands of the eighteenth and nineteenth centuries needed no revolution. That it was still affected was the result of old accounts which had to be settled with the most prominent and arrogant rulers. Adherents of the revolution were labeled patriots. But what were they fighting against? The power of the stadtholders was limited, power was in the hands of the citizens and the towns, so what was there still to be liberated in the Netherlands? The great differences between rich and poor provided a sufficient breeding ground for revolution.

Napoleon and Joséphine

Anyone studying the history of gardens comes up against the name of Joséphine de Beauharnais (1762–1814). Born in Martinique to a highly placed French father and an Italian mother, her beauty was widely renowned in her own time. And what a time: as the mother of two children, she saw her husband, the Count de Beauharnais, go to his death by the guillotine as a member of the aristocracy. The same fate threatened her and her two daughters. After many vicissitudes she became the mistress of Napoleon Bonaparte, the leader of the French revolutionary government, which had declared war on the established order and on the rules accepted up to that time. In 1796 they were married. Both Napoleon and Joséphine have influenced the prosperity of the tulip, each in his and her individual way.

Above: *Tulipa* **'Early Glory'**.

Below: **'Maywonder'** under the flowering crab apple *Malus floribunda*.

An admirable arrangement of water-loving plants, rhododendrons, and 'Page Polka' tulips.

A new style of garden

Le style Anglais is one of the achievements of the French Revolution. New rulers, members of the Bonaparte family, were sent to the conquered countries as kings or queens of Italy, the Netherlands, and Spain. With the politicians and the generals, they were the new rich. They built grand houses in a "democratic" style inspired by Greek temples: Neo-classicism. They had their houses furnished in the entirely new Empire style, and broke away from the formal French garden designs. It is known that Napoleon did not like the gardens at Versailles, but fortunately, out of respect for Louis XIV, whom he admired as a great statesman and general, he did not have those gardens altered into

the style then popular, the English style. Many formal gardens in France were transformed into English gardens, with wide lawns, random groups of trees, a lake, a few pavilions, a graceful bridge, and some flower gardens near the house. Joséphine had a garden like this laid out at Malmaison, her country house near Paris.

The Bois de Boulogne is another magnificent example of a landscape garden, in this case an enormous park with fine lakes, meandering paths, and tracks for walkers and riders. In the Bois de Boulogne is the Bagatelle, designed by the Scottish garden architect Thomas Blaikie.

This was the result of a wager by the Count of Artois, an active supporter of the French Revolution; he bet that a garden could be laid out in the Bois de Boulogne, complete, within one month.

He won, and the result was a splendid landscaped park with pavilions, water, and wide lawns. Later, roses were planted there, and now, together with l'Häy des Roses, also in Paris, it is the national rose museum. Modern roses are in the Bagatelle; in l'Häy des Roses, in the Anthony district in south Paris, are the old roses admired by Joséphine. She also loved tulips and had them painted by the flower painter Redouté, whom in fact she discovered, and who was to gain great renown from them.

Redouté, flower painter *par excellence*

The Belgian painter Pierre Joseph Redouté (1759–1840) had come to Paris as an up-and-coming artist to gain experience in painting landscapes. His passion for gambling meant that this able painter was always in need of money, and he therefore accepted, although at first unwillingly, the Empress Joséphine's request to draw her tulips and other flowers. It was not the first time that artists from the northern and southern Netherlands had traveled to Paris to paint flowers for the court. This honor had also fallen to the painter Van Spaendonck,

Above: A yellow-white border with the flowering crab apple
Malus floribunda, **and on the left Darwin hybrids**
'Apeldoorns Elite', lily-flowered 'White Triumphator',
and single late 'Magier' tulips.

Left: *Tulipa* **'White Triumphator'.**

and many brilliant works by his hand were the result. Redouté's talent for engraving flowers, and later coloring in the prints by hand, earned him a great deal of money. Yet he was obliged to keep at it, as the money he earned was very soon frittered away. Consequently, we can now enjoy a unique collection of paintings, which give a wonderful picture of the varieties then in use in arrangements and in gardens.

A farm garden designed by the author. The whole back garden is filled with white flowers: here white Darwin tulips. To the left and right of the old fruit trees are borders of white perennials, including roses.

The Lille flower dealers

In the nineteenth century, dealers from Limmen and from the bulbfields near Hillegom and Lisse exported enormous quantities of tulips to many countries in Europe. They were not, however, the only ones. The cultivation of tulips also flourished in Belgium and northern France. Lille was then completely Flemish-speaking. The dealers were active in inventing special new varieties, and built up a large clientele at the French court and among the prominent rich bourgeoisie. A Monsieur Tripet exhibited more than 800 varieties at a Paris flower show in 1843. Sadly, the Lille tulip trade came to an end, and no more bulbs are grown there now. The incorporation of Lille into France gradually brought an end to the use of Dutch as the general written and

spoken language, and the region became totally French. Now it is a "boom town" with industry on the sites where tulips once bloomed.

Growing bulbs from seed

The Lille bulb growers made great improvements to the type known as Darwin tulips, and invented many new varieties by repeatedly fertilizing the stamen of one variety with pollen from another, waiting until the seed was mature, and then sowing it. It took six years for the tiny seed to develop into a full-grown bulb. The consequence was that these bulb growers could produce the best stock, and could stipulate top prices for their tulips. Darwin tulips, grown by M.J. Lenglart of Lille, are currently the most common tulips on the market. Their popularity, which has steadily increased since the arrival of this division in 1886, is due to their rather rounded shape. Most Darwin tulips bloom fairly late, in May, and have long straight stems.

The tulip trade in Belgium and the north of France declined toward the end of the nineteenth century, and was ousted by the cultivation of azaleas and tuberous begonias, bay, and other plants, grown particularly in the Ghent area. Fortunately, the collection of Darwin tulips was saved, together with many other types and varieties of tulips created in Flanders and grown there. They were bought by Krelage, the Haarlem bulb grower.

The Darwin hybrids were grown later by Lefebre, the Dutch grower.

Left: Tulips in a well-composed design.

Above: The Triumph tulip 'Valentine' in an informal border.

Below: 'Pink Impression' in a massed planting.

CHAPTER II

Tulips in the Early 20th Century

A great deal of pioneering work has been done by Dutch growers in their search for new, as yet undiscovered varieties. Russia, too, has made its contribution.

Russia, the St. Petersburg botanic garden

In 1855 August von Regel, a famous German botanist, was appointed horticultural director of the botanic garden in St. Petersburg. He applied himself to his task with exemplary industry, and put in hand many expeditions to search for new wild tulips in southern Russia. Military operations provided the opportunity to collect tulips from Turkmenistan, Uzbekistan, Tajikistan, Armenia, and the Caucasus. From Turkmenistan in particular came flowers which have greatly influenced the diversity of our range of tulips, and which are still popular as very early flowering blooms. They were *Tulipa kaufmanniana*, *eichleri*, and *greigii*.

This delightful spring display greets the passer-by with its delicate shades. 'Apeldoorn' is combined with low-growing yellow *Alyssum saxatile* and *Doronicum orientale* to the right of the yellow broom. This kind of effect best suits country cottages and farmhouses, where bright primary colors can be set beside the green grass and blue sky with which they have to compete.

Van Tubergen's tulips

Van Tubergen, the Dutch grower, sent many botanical expeditions to distant countries in Asia and Asia Minor to look for special tulips, and some of these discoveries turned out to be unexpectedly important. P. Graeber, a German living in Tashkent, found an unknown tulip there which was grown on as *T. tubergeniana*. He also discovered *T. hoogiana*, named after Van Tubergen's joint manager, as well as *T. batalinii* and *T. linifolia*, which grows with a narrow leaf. Paul Sintenis was an Austrian botanist who sent *T. wilsonii* from Asia Minor to Van Tubergen's nursery in Haarlem. In Samarkand Joseph Habenhauer found *T. fosteriana*, named after Foster, the famous British botanist and plant hunter. George Egger, a German plant hunter in Tabriz, sent *T. lantans* to the Netherlands. The importance of

This sun-filled *Tulipa fosteriana* 'Yellow purissima' drives away all dullness, mist, and rain. The color can be repeated in other taller or shorter tulips, and always looks best in small, meandering groups in flower borders.

these finds is shown by the results of crossing the wild species with a cultivated one, the Darwin tulip. From this came the Darwin hybrids which are now so popular.

The man who sent all these expeditions to China, Tibet, India, the Soviet Union, and Asia Minor, was Tom M. Hoog, joint manager of Van Tubergen's. With remarkable foresight he expanded the range of tulip varieties enormously. The new species could be used to create hybrids, and the range of tulips grew ever more various. As well as Hoog, his contemporary J.F.C. Dix also made an increasingly important contribution. Dix worked in the nursery of

The flower garden of this farm house has been integrated with the kitchen garden.

This border resembles a Persian carpet, sparkling with pink, orange, red, and yellow. The tall flowers are crown imperial (*Fritillaria*).

a famous bulb grower, Dr. Ernst Krelage. Krelage bought a large collection of Flemish tulips in 1886. Moreover, he was the man who introduced scientific methods to the culture and propagation of bulbs. With his successor, Hoog, Dix helped a great deal to research new methods of propagation, to create new hybrids, and finally, to make great improvements to the quality of the bulbs. They achieved a world-renowned product for the horticultural market which still commands keen demand throughout the world.

Dutch tulips in Turkey

The tulip remained the favorite flower of the Turkish court. Sultan Ahmet III (1673–1736) had tulips imported from Holland to add to his large collection. He held great tulip festivals to which he invited foreign guests. The French ambassador,

J.P. Ardène, has left us a description of the important role played by the tulip in the life of the Turkish rulers. The Tulip Festival in Istanbul is a reminder of this eighteenth-century pomp, which is still celebrated, unfortunately without tulips! Ahmet was deposed by the Janissaries and died in prison, but fortunately his successors continued to be interested in tulips. So tulips returned to the land that had first presented their bulbs to the Flemish ambassador de Busbecq. The shape of the Dutch tulips that were now reaching Turkey was quite different from the narrow, lean, almond-shaped Turkish tulips of so long ago, demonstrating how successfully they had been grown on.

Tulips in the nineteenth-century gardens

Left: This entrance takes us spellbound along a half circle, embellished with yellow-red tulips and *Alyssum saxatile*.
Right: Here the true red 'Apeldoorn' tulip has been used.

Le style mixte, or mixed style, is used for a type of garden which combines both landscape and more formal elements. After the fashion for grandiose park landscapes, which swept over Europe and America, the need was felt for a greater variation, not only in a profusion of flowers, but also in design. No longer did people want to see just lawns, lakes, stands of trees, and variations in contours, but they also longed for new flower gardens with areas for exotic plants, for greenhouses, and for more variation in layout. Circular beds with roses or annuals came into fashion, with all the shapes deriving from them, such as ellipses, festoons, and kidney shapes. Statues were again placed near water basins, and rose arches, rose gardens, box gardens, and specialist gardens were added to the greenhouses.

One of the most attractive gardens of that time, recently restored to all its old glory, and one in which there are many tulips, is the impressionist painter Claude Monet's garden at Giverny in France. The garden is in two parts, separated by a public road. The oldest part is directly behind the long house; it is divided into long paths and flower beds running at right angles to the house. A central graveled path leads straight from the back door of the house to a gate giving access to the garden from the public road. In the spring there are tulips all along this path, as there are in fact all over the garden. They are nowadays selected more or less by

color, and planted together with violets, daisies,
and wallflowers in the same yellow, white, pink, or
deep orange-red colors. Clever combinations have
been made in these gardens of patches of color
lying next to each other, which even now form the
polychromatic entity which must have been so
essential to Monet's sense of beauty. In his garden
paintings, the rich mixture of colors, made up of
purple, red, yellow, and blue, stands out. He did not
paint gardens with delicate colors, but a profusion
of color, which inspired the master to many of his
most magnificent oil paintings. In summer, when the
tulips and other spring flowers are over, there are
peonies, eremus, roses in abundance, many kinds of
irises, lilies, and all the annuals of Monet's time.
Nasturtiums planted along the main path spill in
great lobes over it, and make it almost impossible to
walk along the path.

Many painters and gardeners go into raptures at the sight of this field full of Parrot tulips.

Monet and the tulip fields

The discovery of the Dutch bulbfields must have
been an overwhelming experience for this artist. His
trip to the Netherlands included a visit to the area of
De Zaan, where he found his inspiration for the use
of green paint, used there on the old wooden houses,
for his house at Giverny. He used the summer
cottages built along the River Zaan as a subject for
his paintings, but the greatest impact was made by
the completely flat fields planted with brilliant
colored strips of bulbs alongside each other. The
endless distant prospects, with an occasional village,
a windmill, the clear skies with their blues and

evening reds, inspired him to a series of colorful paintings which stand quite apart from the rest of his œuvre. These paintings have linked tulips with this artist, and he became one of the many world-famous painters who were inspired by them.

White tulips in Dieppe

In the early twentieth century the Mallet family of French bankers laid out a fine garden that has been cherished and improved for three generations. The grandfather of the present owner gave the initial impetus by building a summer residence on the coast, looking across the Channel at his beloved England. The Mallets were very interested in art and literature, and asked several artists, including an architect and a garden designer from England, to help with the construction and interior decoration, and the design of their new garden near Dieppe. The architect was the then relatively unknown Edwin Lutyens, and the garden designer Gertrude Jekyll. Several of the pre-Raphaelites were invited to embellish the interior with tapestries and murals.

Much of the interior has been destroyed by fire, while occupation by the Germans did not exactly improve the once so magnificently decorated house. The atmosphere is, however, still the same, and a few splendid tapestries survived the blaze.

Above: One of the wild tulips still obtainable is *Tulipa sylvestris* (syn. *biebersteiniana*).

Tulips in garden rooms

At the front, the street-side of the house, a series of garden rooms of various sizes have been created by building walls out at right angles to the façade. A narrow strip has been laid out as an entrance garden between the access to the public road and the main entry to the house, with a central path between two wide strips of lawn, and splendid borders planted along each side. Then there is a peaceful white garden beside the large sitting room. This room with a southern aspect is two stories high, and light floods in from the white garden. It is really a courtyard with plenty of paving and beds for roses; white roses, between which tall white 'Triumphator' tulips are planted each spring. They produce a sparkling effect which is later taken over by the roses. Roses also grow against the walls.

The third garden is the scented garden, lying on the other side of the entrance garden, and planted with a profusion of all kinds of aromatic plants. These three linked gardens, separated from each other by walls, reveal the master-hand of Edwin Lutyens who in his subsequent career was the architect of many well-known country houses, as well as the gentle mastery of Gertrude Jekyll. Their partnership in many projects contributed to the renown of both.

'Jessica' is an old-fashioned tulip, which can be seen growing in the wind and spring sunshine in the bulb museum of the Hortus Bulborum.

The back garden

An enormous lawn flows from the back of the house, which has a completely different atmosphere and style, to a mysterious-looking wood. On the left there are Japanese azaleas and large beech trees, and some blue *Cedrus atlantica 'glauca'*. On the right is a path with tree heathers, rhododendrons, and many gray-leaved and purple-flowered shrubs. A path leads to the wood, where a lot has been done with light and contrasting foliage. For instance, there is a rhododendron glade, and there are moist areas where rodgersias and ferns display their fine foliage. Deeper in the wood you can see the chalk cliffs indicating the geological fault which arose when France and England split apart. However, the wood is dense, and the coast dangerous, so that access to both garden and wood is restricted.

The Beukenhof in Oegstgeest

Not many tulips are planted each year in the garden of the celebrated restaurant De Beukenhof in Oegstgeest, the Netherlands, but they are no less effective for that. Few gardens suggest such an atmosphere of early twentieth-century England as the Lutyens-inspired garden of De Beukenhof. The designer was Leonard van der Putten, who spent many years in England studying the new garden styles of Gertrude Jekyll and Harold Robinson, and Sir Edwin Lutyens' architectural ideas.

Near Limmen's beautiful church grow historic tulips, daffodils, scillas, lady's smock, crown imperials, and hyacinths; all collected by Dutch plantsmen since the fifteenth century. Fortunately they have not been lost.

Above: *Tulipa* **'Menton'.**

Below: 'Apricot Beauty', a single early tulip.

England was then in the grip of the "arts and crafts" movement, which had visions of providing a counterbalance to the all-pervasive industrialization. With this objective the movement, under the leadership of William Morris, encouraged the establishment of workshops for weaving, hand-blocked wallpapers, jewelry, and furniture to original designs. This movement, which encouraged a return to craftsmanship, resulted in a style for buildings which can be recognizably rustic, and a revival of the friendly cottage style. Antique roses over a barn, plants growing in jumbled profusion, a festive display, and materials for paths, pergolas, and walls suggesting that they had been gnawed by centuries of wear, were then popular among designers of both large and small gardens.

In the Netherlands Van der Putten developed the ideas he had gleaned in England in his own garden at De Beukenhof, and in a number of private gardens across the country. Fixed elements were pergolas with masonry pillars bearing wooden cross members. The brick pillars were usually left unpainted, though this is not the case at De Beukenhof, perhaps in an attempt to introduce a white element in the garden to match the old white hostelry. The pavement is a mix of English flagstones with brick paving, and the garden is divided by numerous hedges.

These long houses combined with stables are to be found in many regions of the Netherlands, and their own traditional gardens are still cherished. Here the red Triumph tulip 'Paul Richter' with *Alyssum* and *Doronicum*, proven favorites around Easter when yellow is a popular color.

tari) are used between the tulips
nd intensifying element of color.
, as do pansies in white, yellow,

Daffodils, hyacinths, enormous
s, and fields of blue grape
nges between groups of tulips,
planted in harmonious com-
nes in deliberately "shocking"
to create an integrated whole
r round branching shapes, the
he landscaped park, and the
f the pools and groups of tulips.
en very successfully achieved.
ls and expanses of lawn mean
profusion of tulips is visible at

f

A long pool, regrettably recently somewhat reduced in length, runs past the restaurant into the depths of the garden, where it makes a right-angled bend repeated by the pergola. Alongside this pool tulips flower in pots each spring, dazzlingly beautiful and inspiring in their simplicity. Busts of gods and goddesses placed between them give a rhythm to the edges of the pool. This simple use of tulips deserves more imitation, and proves that an excellent effect can be produced with tulips quite inexpensively. Mr. Werner, the gardener who has worked here more than thirty years, plants the bulbs at the end of the summer, so that they can develop in their pots. A good idea, because in this way the tulips flower for longer than when they are potted out as fully grown bulbs, almost ready to flower.

Above: 'Graf Zeppelin'.

Below: *Tulipa* 'Keizerskroon', a museum piece.

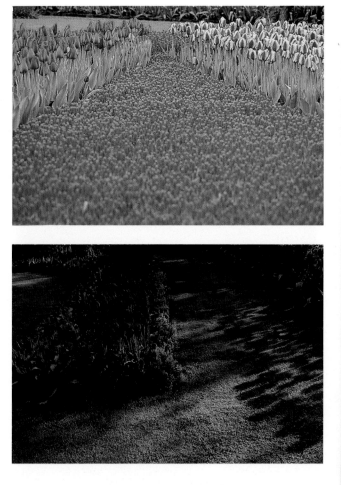

Above 'Gordon Cooper' and 'Apeldoorns Elite'.
Below: The single late tulip 'Red Georgette'.

In view of the obvious enjoyment of many thousands of visitors, this approach can be judged a success. To prevent too much uniformity, the Keukenhof design team has created extensive theme gardens: a white garden, a Japanese garden, a rock garden, and many other types, and have integrated tulips most appropriately into them. These theme gardens can be an inspiration for your own garden, quite an achievement in such a large park. It is a good idea to have a specific objective when visiting the Keukenhof: for example, to look out for appealing color combinations. Everything is labeled, so that you can make a note of these combinations, and the particulars of their height, type and shape of flower, variety, and type of bulb suitable for your own garden. From this point of view the Keukenhof can be a fount of inspiration for amateur gardeners. We all have our own ideas about the use of bulbs in a

Primary colors go with blue skies, plenty of bright green grass, and yellow marigolds along the waterside. The color combination is particularly suitable for farmhouses and simple architecture.

garden, and some garden lovers are put off by the great range of colors and abundance of bulbs. If the Keukenhof is regarded as a sample garden available for research and study, it becomes a wonderfully informative garden, which can give visitors a great deal of very useful information, as well as much aesthetic pleasure.

When the bulbs have been lifted and the park is left empty and without its extra colors, a miracle occurs: the trees are in full leaf, the grass is green, the water gray-green and blue, and the park returns to the peace and tranquility which reigns here for all seasons except spring.

Some impressive special displays

On entering the Keukenhof, one is immediately confronted with a brilliant picture to left and right. An almost endless streak of blue grape hyacinths is drawn like a narrow blue line through fresh green lawns. The line runs between rows of lime trees, and is a most striking example of the use of bulbs and flowers. From here long lanes take the visitor through the woods with pools, statues, and ever-changing combinations of color.

The theme gardens are a welcome change from the many landscaped plantings of tulips, daffodils, and hyacinths. The constantly recurring use of rows, fields, and accents of blue grape hyacinths, which both neutralize and intensify the color of the other bulbs, is striking. In the theme gardens various kinds of garden styles have been translated into real

In the oldest part of the English park theme landscape in the celebrated Keukenhof bulb garden there are winding paths, pools, and slopes. Near the entrance all is in straight lines, as in a polder landscape.

gardens to demonstrate the many ways in which bulbs can be used. For this purpose wide paths have been laid out so that visitors can examine everything closely without doing any damage. There are also quite tiny gardens, among which the white garden is a miracle of diversity. A pot garden under a canopy is a gesture to those who garden on a balcony or a terrace. There is much to see, particularly some very fine ornaments, consisting not only of well-sited statues, but also pots and troughs. The tall lead plant containers arranged near the water garden are also appealing and draw the eye to this section of the garden as a closing feature.

Above: Often an exhibiting bulb firm is allotted a small section of ground for its latest varieties.

Below: Here people can choose the colors most suitable for their own gardens.

Anyone wishing to see the whole garden should allow at least an entire day for the Keukenhof; for residents in the Netherlands it makes more sense to study the early, normal, and late-flowering bulbs on several separate visits. For anyone wanting to plant bulbs, the Keukenhof is a must, though every garden designer will probably want to incorporate his own ideas on the alternation and variety of bulbs to be displayed in his own garden.

Perhaps a little of the space covered by the Keukenhof could be set aside for samples of such designs, and serve as a trendsetter in which leading Dutch gardening experts could show examples of their ideas, which in turn could be an additional stimulus for the bulb trade.

CHAPTER 13

Tulips Old and New

A list of tulips, broken down by flowering season, is a useful aid for anyone wanting to grow them in their own garden. If you follow this scheme, successive groups of tulips will flower for months on end. (This analysis by flowering season cuts across the official divisions of the Royal Dutch and the English Horticultural Societies.)

Above: In a spring garden it is important to combine tulips with fresh foliage. Here the wine red underside of *Ligularia dentata* 'Desdemona' is combined with white lily-flowered 'White Triumphator' (number 9) and the yellow single late tulip 'Mrs J.T. Scheepers'. Above is the flowering crab apple *Malus toringo* var. *sargentii*.

Right: Number 3 tulips, double early tulips, can be admired in a wealth of color in the Keukenhof.

Group A: early-flowering tulips

Number 1

The finest in this group are the sixteenth- and seventeenth-century tulips cultivated by the Leiden grower Van Tol. These varieties are in the Dutch national plant collection, and are therefore protected as national property. The Hortus Bulborum is charged with the care of these centuries-old species of tulips. Small quantities of all varieties are grown on, planted out, and exhibited in flower in straight beds, where they can be seen by visitors. The 'Duc van Tol' varieties are low, early-flowering, and brightly colored, a real treat for plant lovers interested in historical species. They were sadly absent from Jefferson's Monticello garden, but they can fortunately be seen in William and Mary's Dutch garden at Het Loo. Small quantities of old species or varieties of tulips can usually be made available for owners of historic gardens, but they are not grown on a commercial scale.

Number 2

These are early-flowering single tulips which have evolved from a cross between *Tulipa gesneriana* and *T. suaveolens*. The original old varieties have short stems and are bright yellow and red. Modern varieties with tall stems are now also available in many colors. This group is also used in glasshouses for forcing, and provides early cut flowers.

The tulips complete with bulbs, grown in baskets in large quantities for Christmas, also come from this group.

Number 3

The double early tulips make up this group. The flowers are large, often resembling a peony in shape and size. These somewhat old-fashioned, but endearing, early tulips, usually low-growing, can be enjoyed in the garden in April. There are some fine shades of pink and white, and many shades of yellow.

Group B: mid-April to mid-May

Number 4

This group is represented by the Mendel tulips, which originated in a cross between the later Darwin tulips and the sixteenth-century 'Duc van Tol' described in number 1. They were produced in 1920 by one of the well-known Dutch growers, Dr. E.H. Krelage. Some time earlier Krelage had bought up the Darwin tulip in Lille, and by doing so had rescued this influential, and now so important species of tulip from extinction. There are some beautiful Mendel tulips on the market, among them the popular and aptly named 'Apricot Beauty'. There are, however, also red, pink, violet, and white varieties available beside the yellow Mendel varieties. They are strong, long-stemmed tulips, frequently used in planting.

Number 5

The Triumph tulips in this group flower as early as April. They are the result of a cross between the Darwin tulip and the tulips described in number 2, the single early varieties. They are grown by N. Zandbergen of the Rijnsburg company. This tulip, resistant to bad weather, rain, and wind, and with a fairly short stem, was introduced in 1933, and marketed in a wide range of colors. The flowers are larger than those of the Mendel tulip, number 4, and more compact, because of their short stems.

Above: Number 2:
the single early tulip 'Prins Carnaval'.

Right: Number 4:
the single early tulip 'Apricot Beauty'.

Group C: late-flowering tulips

This group includes Darwin tulips which are at the moment the most popular. Special species and varieties, such as the Parrot tulips, are also in this group, as well as the lily-flowered tulips, which sometimes are seen to closely resemble the Triumph tulips.

Number 6

Darwin tulips are known to every tulip lover. It is a blow to the pride of Dutch bulb growers that this very strong flower was invented not by a Dutch grower, but by a French one. M.J. Lenglart, an amateur grower, produced this bulb at the end of the nineteenth century. He crossed various tulips with each other, in particular Cottage tulips, so called because they evolved in English cottage gardens. The sturdy flowers are wide at the bottom, and somewhat narrower at the top. Darwins flower in May in the northern hemisphere. In the countries of the southern hemisphere these tulips flower after the European summer is over, and are planted during the European spring.

More unusual, and less well-known, is the almost black Darwin tulip, named 'Queen of the Night'. The color is not a true black, but deep purple. There are also striped Darwin tulips, suitable for arrangements in seventeenth-century style, such as *Tulipa* 'American Flag'. Its flower has red and white stripes, or is flecked. Also on the market are various shades of white, soft yellow, orange-yellow, violet, white and violet, and red in many nuances, resulting from the unremitting efforts of the growers of Darwin tulips.

Number 7

This group owes its existence to crossing Darwin tulips with *Tulipa fosteriana* 'Red Emperor', resulting in Darwin hybrids. This was done by the well-known grower D.W. Lefebre with so much success that the Darwin hybrids are considered by many to be the most important innovation of the last few decades. In 1936 'Madame Lefebre' was introduced, the result of crossing the common Darwin tulip with *T. fosteriana*, and this bloom, with its slimmer profile, has proved to be a good counterpart for the Darwin varieties themselves. Splendid violet and satin red shades were inherited from the *T. fosteriana*. Well-known varieties include 'Elizabeth Arden', a pale violet, and 'Spring Song', a brighter violet with a narrower constriction at the top, a wide base of petals, and a round pointed tip. *T.* 'Beauty of Apeldoorn' is orange, with red stripes. The success story of 'Apeldoorn' is well-known: it is probably the best known flower for cutting and for the garden, and can easily be identified by its firm, red flowers. Its sister is the yellow *T.* 'Golden Apeldoorn'. This successful group of tulips has not yet seen the end of its triumphal progress.

Right: Number 7:

the Darwin hybrid 'Beauty of Apeldoorn'.

Left: Number 6:

the single late tulip 'Queen of Night'.

Below: Number 18:

the *fosteriana* tulip 'Orange Emperor'.

Number 8

This popular group, known as Breeder tulips, is a particular favorite with real garden lovers. The flowers resemble the Darwin, and show a large variety of colors, which will attract many people. These tulips are tall-stemmed and strong, and can have any color to suit your planting scheme.

Number 9

The lily-flowered tulips are a great favorite of many. They have exceptionally graceful long, pointed petals, which sometimes bend a little outwards. They meet what is believed to have been the ideal for the tulips in the Ottoman gardens of the sixteenth to eighteenth centuries, when their beautiful almond shape was an aesthetic requirement. The stems of this tulip are long, and tend to bend when at their full height, until they collapse in a tangle of stems. They need to be planted in a sunny spot, sheltered from the wind. Pink, white, and yellow shades are available. They were produced by the famous grower Krelage.

The lily shape was derived from a cross between *Tulipa retroflexa* and an English Cottage tulip (number 10). It is not known who cultivated the specific Cottage tulip involved, but *T. retroflexa* was raised by V. van der Winnen, who in 1863 crossed *T. gesneriana* with *T. acuminata*.

The success of the 'Triumphator' varieties is due to their elegance: graceful flowers on tall stems. Especially 'White Triumphator', the white, lily-flowered tulip, is magnificent in pots, or planted between tall lavender, bergenia, and gray santolina. It is also a "must" in pots and flower arrangements.

Right: Number 10:

the single late tulip 'Rosy Wings'.

Number 10

This large group of tulips originally came from English cottage gardens. It is generally known what is meant by cottage gardens: small bright gardens, with a mixture of herbs, annuals, perennials, roses, and here and there an ornamental shrub. These are the gardens of devotees who are averse to any kind of formal style. Cottages, often originally occupied by poor labourers, had small rooms and windows, and sometimes thatched roofs; they now frequently belong to retired people. Their gardens can provide a real treasure trove for anyone looking for old-fashioned plants. Because generations of gardening enthusiasts have exchanged cottage plants with each other, taken cuttings, and cross-fertilized, many old plants have survived. Similarly the tulips in these gardens were pollinated spontaneously by bees, or through a love for propagation by the occupants of the cottages, achieving crosses between their plants and their neighbor's. This group is not uniform, but still shows a certain identity which it did not have in the past. The flower of the Cottage tulip is generally as wide at the base as at the top, the tulip has a tall stem, and is available in many single colors, as well as mixed color combinations. 'Rosy Wings' and 'Burgundy Lace' are a lilac color. 'Greenland' is pink, with a green flame which narrows towards the top. 'Princess Margaret Rose' is not pink, but yellow, except at the tips of the petals, which are bright red.

Left: in the lily-flowered tulips (number 9)

there is also great variation.

Number 11

These typically Dutch tulips date from the seventeenth century, and are known as Rembrandt tulips. Their flowers show the broken color, sometimes striped, sometimes flecked, so popular during the Golden Age of Holland. They have now lost their mass appeal, and some gardening enthusiasts reject these tulips which were so often the prized models for paintings in the past. And to think that in the sixteenth and seventeenth centuries people were prepared to pay thousands of guilders for a bulb that could produce such flowers! It is now known that striped tulips were the result of a viral disease which was very contagious and often fatal to the bulb. For this reason bulbs with a viral disease are no longer cultivated – they are even destroyed. However, careful cultivation of Darwin tulips has at last made it possible to offer striped and flecked varieties, so that flower arrangements in a more or less authentic seventeenth-century style can again be produced.

Number 12

The main color of the tulips in this group is yellow; they are named 'Bizarre'. This group can be identified by the brown to purple stripes on the yellow petals. 'Bizarre' is derived by crossing with the Breeder tulip (number 8) or the Cottage tulip (number 10).

Number 13

This tulip resembles number 12, and has white petals. Red, violet, or pink stripes or flecks can be seen on their petals. These flowers for connoisseurs are beautiful in out-of-the ordinary or old-style arrangements.

Number 14

The Parrot tulip is a delight for all slightly decadent flower lovers. Scorned by many, and beloved by specialists in antiquity and by flower arrangers, these flowers, first introduced in 1665, are easily identified. The petals curl outwards at the top, and are often fringed at the edges. There are many monochrome and mixed-color combinations. 'Black Parrot' is deep purple, 'Texas Gold' is yellow. 'Flaming Parrot' is white with a red stripe through the middle of each petal, and there are many more variations. 'Blue Parrot' can be recommended to anyone who is hankering after a "civilized" Parrot tulip, although it is not blue (alas), but a beautiful purple violet color. There is, however, one disadvantage to the Parrot tulip: at the time of flowering the stems are tall and the flowers large, and as a result they often bend. This makes it necessary to pick the tulip if its beauty is to be appreciated to the full. It is therefore more suitable as a tulip for cutting or as a pot plant, where a support can be provided for each flower. And for a gift, one flower easily suffices!

Below left: Number 11:

the single late tulip 'Union Jack'.

Below right: Number 14:

the Parrot tulip 'Flaming Parrot'.

Group D: Botanical tulips

Number 15

This group consists of double late-flowering tulips. They flower in the second half of May, and offer a splendid sight alongside azaleas in the same shade. These tulips, too, are vulnerable because of their large, double flowers, which resemble peonies. However, their splendour as cut flowers in the house makes it easy to overlook this drawback.

All these numbered groups of tulips have evolved as a result of endless cross fertilization, selection, and research – achieved by human hand, in fact! The remaining groups should be distinguished from them because they are directly identifiable wild or botanical tulips, or crosses from them.

Opposite: Number 3:

the double early tulip 'Peach Blossom'.

Below: Number 15:

the double late tulip 'Angelique'.

Number 16

Tulipa batalinii has produced a cross: the bronze-coloured *T*. 'Bronze Charm'. This tulip evolved from the crossing of *T. batalinii* with *T. linifolia*.

Number 17

Tulipa eichleri has bright red flowers, like the *T. e.* 'Excelsa' variety grown by Van Tubergen, but 'Excelsa' has larger red flowers, which look an even brighter red when they grow in the garden.

Number 18

Tulipa fosteriana is one of the most important ancestors of the Darwin hybrids, which come from a cross between *fosteriana* and an unknown Cottage tulip (see number 7). The bright to deep red color is characteristic, as is the large size of the flowers. There are several varieties on the market of this botanical tulip, in various shades of red.

Number 19

Tulipa greigii has multicolored flowers. Orange or purple red shades are often visible in the petals, which are usually black at the base, with a yellow edge. There are, however, many varieties descended from the original of this tulip; many other tulips have also been crossed with *T. greigii*, producing a wide variety of both shapes and colors in their progeny.

Number 20

Tulipa kaufmanniana is perhaps one of the most popular early-flowering bulbs in the Netherlands. This tulip was found in Turkmenistan, as were *T. eichleri* (number 17) and *T. greigii* (number 19). August von Regel (1815–92), curator of the imperial botanic gardens in St. Petersburg, was a great tulip hunter; Turkmenistan was the objective of the expeditions he made with his son and other botanists. *Kaufmanniana* is the first tulip to flower, a delight in the garden with its low stem, sometimes producing a single color, sometimes more. 'Stresa' is one of the multi-colored varieties, and is yellow with large red triangles on the petals. 'Heart's Delight' is a pinkish red variety, which is a very pale pink inside, a beautiful combination. There are now many varieties of *kaufmanniana* on the market; all of them are low-stemmed and flower in March – an asset in any garden. There are also crosses with *T. greigii* (number 19), flecked with brown or white.

Below: number 20:

Tulipa kaufmanniana 'Stresa'.

Number 21

A completely separate group of tulips are the *Neo-tulipae*. The name here is *Tulipa marjolettii*. One man, Abbot Fritsch, is responsible for saving the almost extinct wild tulips from Savoy in France. He knew where in Chambéry there were wild tulips which had attracted his attention as a botanist, and which according to him had never been described. To his dismay the area was designated for building. Despite his request, building went ahead, and he had to dig out the last bulbs before the bulldozers moved in. These bulbs he grew on in Chambéry, so that a few of them, which are known as *Neo-tulipae* in the botanical world, and grow to a height of 20 in (50 cm), were saved for tulip lovers.

Other wild tulips have been described in such places as Susa in north-west Italy, where *T. sequesteriana* was found, while *grengiolensis* was discovered in Valais, Switzerland. T. Thommen described this wild species as recently as 1946. Experts are not agreed on whether *Neo-tulipae* are genuine wild species which have ended up in northern Italy and neighboring Savoy via Macedonia and former Yugoslavia, or whether they are "escaped" garden species which have maintained themselves and multiplied outside gardens. But there is every reason to be grateful for Abbot Fritsch's actions, which have earned him a place in the annals of the tulip.

Number 22

This group is named after the Haarlem bulb growers Van Tubergen: *Tulipa tubergeniana*. This wild tulip was found by P.L. Graeber in Tashkent in the former Soviet Union, near the border of Afghanistan. The name of this vast area is Tajikistan; plant hunters sent out by Van Tubergen went there in the spring to look for fields of wild tulips. Graeber lived in Tashkent from 1880 to 1914, and found *T. tubergeniana*, as well as *T. hoogiana* (named after Van Tubergen's joint manager), *T. ingens*, *T. linifolia*, and *T. batalinii*. *T. tubergeniana* is bright red in color and flowers early. New late-flowering hybrids have been developed by crossing this wild tulip with Darwin tulips.

Apart from these well-known botanical tulips many others are more or less easily obtainable, and well worth collecting by tulip enthusiasts.

Right: Number 26:

Tulipa praestans 'Fusilier'.

Number 23

In the first instance this is *Tulipa clusiana*, which in 1607 flowered in the botanic garden at Leiden in the Netherlands. The flower is striped violet and white on the outside, and white inside. It is long in shape. Originally it came from Afghanistan, Persia, and Iraq. This tulip grows in gardens along all the coasts of the Mediterranean. It is nicknamed Lady Tulip. The bulb can be left in the ground, and flowers if it is planted to a depth of 6–8 in (15–20 cm) in well-drained soil.

Right: Number 26:

Tulipa praestans 'Tubergen's Variety'.

Group E: European tulips

Number 24

Tulipa celsiana is a tulip which grows wild in Europe. It was found in southern Spain. The bulb bears several flowers on one stem. Each flower is pale yellow on the inside, red on the outside, and spreads wide open like a star. This tulip multiplies quickly and is also found in Morocco and the Atlas mountains.

Number 25

Tulipa sylvestris also occurs in the wild in Europe and has an important place in the Dutch *stinse* flora; they can be found in the gardens of country houses and of large farms. The flower is long in shape and golden yellow, the leaves are narrow and long, and if the plant is given a reasonably sunny place, its progress will be easy to follow. A must for every garden!

Number 26

Tulipa praestans blooms in early April with beautiful red flowers. This is an easy tulip, flowering year after year, provided it is in a sunny site in rich soil.

Number 27

Another European tulip is *Tulipa praecox*, found wild in the south of France in Provence, the Rhône valley, and Languedoc. These red flowers have a clear identification mark: at the base of the petals there is a green stripe, edged with yellow. They are found also near Bologna in Italy, and on the island of Chios in the Aegean.

Number 28

Tulipa hageri is as European as *T. praestans*. These shortish brown to red and purple flowers are found on Mount Parnassus in Greece and near Smyrna in Turkey.

Number 29

Tulipa australis grows wild along the coast of the Mediterranean and in Portugal. In France it has been found in Provence, Languedoc, and the Maritime Alps; in Italy in the Appenines; and also in Sicily. It has also been found in Algeria, Tripolitania, and in wild mountainous areas of Greece and Turkey.

Number 30

Tulipa acuminata comes from Turkey and has in fact also been called the Turkish tulip. In that country, where tulips have been grown by so many generations of tulip lovers, this is a cultivated tulip which has gone wild, and traces its ancestry to *T. gesneriana*. Yellow or red flowers appear in May, and are pointed in shape.

Below left: Number 19:

Tulipa greigii hybrid

'Red Riding Hood'.

Below right: Number 18:

'Orange Emperor', one of the

fosteriana tulips.

Group F: Wild Persian tulips

As well as *Tulipa clusiana*, several wild botanical species belong to this group.

Number 31

Tulipa aucheriana can be classified as a dwarf form. The flower is orange, star-shaped, and brown on the inside. It flowers in April.

Number 32

Tulipa gesneriana flowers throughout Asia Minor; it takes its name from its finder, Gesner. It is assumed that this tulip was the ancestor of our modern tulips. The flower is rather spherical, and scarlet in color. The outside of the petals is slightly paler. Crosses among flowers in the wild have produced other colors, such as red and yellow, without human intervention.

Number 33

Tulipa lanata is one of the brightest colored of the wild botanical tulips still being grown: purple with an olive green heart. A yellow edge is visible like a halo around this green heart. W. Egger, a German living in Tabriz and hunting tulips for Van Tubergen's, found this wild tulip and sent it to them in Haarlem in 1930. Like other botanical tulips, this tulip produces a side root in which a new bulb develops, so that it spreads rapidly.

Number 34

Tulipa polychroma grows in the mountainous regions of Persia. This is perhaps the earliest flowering tulip; it blooms as early as February. It will not grow outside in northern climates unless the bulbs are forced in a glasshouse beforehand. It produces five white flowers on a single stem. Real tulip lovers will certainly want to possess this low-growing tulip.

Number 35

Tulipa sprengeri grows throughout Asia Minor, and also in Persia; its orange-red blooms are the last of all tulips to come into flower in middle to late May. It is also remarkable in that it tolerates shade. This self-seeded tulip increases rapidly in a garden.

Number 36

Tulipa pulchella also occurs in various places in Asia Minor. It is a dwarf tulip with a violet-purple flower. The plant is very suitable for rock gardens or pots, placed close to French windows, or set on a low garden table to display the low-growing flowers.

Below: Number 9:

the lily-flowered tulip 'White Triumphator'.

Left: Number 10:

the fringed tulip 'Burgundy Lace'.

Group G: Turkestan and other countries in Central Asia

Number 37

Tulipa turkestanica produces seven white flowers in May. This small tulip is found in large numbers on its native steppes. There is a yellow fleck at the base of each petal. The flowers of this plant are star-shaped.

Number 38

Tulipa tarda is highly valued by lovers of plant trays and raised gardens. These yellow-white flowers look magnificent both in raised, well-drained plant troughs, and in rock gardens, which have largely disappeared from many modern gardens. The plant increases fast, and will display its six star-shaped blooms in May.

Number 39

Tulipa stellata grows in the mountains of northern India and Afghanistan. The flowers of these tulips, yellow-white inside and red outside, appear in April. The stems are short. Again this is an ideal tulip for plant trays, raised gardens, and rock gardens. To see the tulip in the wild, you must travel to the slopes of the Hindu Kush, where they flower in large quantities in April. *T. praestans* grows in Tajikistan, and its stem bears four smooth red flowers. It is an asset for any garden. It is 12 in (30 cm) high.

Number 40

Tulipa ostrowskiana grows in eastern Turkestan where its purple flowers cover the ground in late April. This is a "forgotten" tulip, which deserves to be introduced by anyone who has the space. The flowers are not large, but provide a good color next to plants such as soapwort (*Saponaria ocymoides*), and will quickly fill ever increasing areas of their flowerbed. *T. ostrowskiana* is identifiable by the small yellow-green fleck below each petal of this 8 in (20 cm) high tulip.

Number 41

Tulipa linifolia grows in Uzbekistan, the republic found to the west of Turkmenistan, where it displays its bright purple flowers, which again are at home in flower troughs, raised trays, and rock gardens. The flower stands about 6 in (15 cm) high. It flowers in May and likes full sun and a warm spot near a fence or hedge.

Number 42

Tulipa kolpakowskiana, which blooms in the steppes near the Aral Sea, and also in the mountains of Tien-Shan in eastern Turkestan, has an unpronounce-able name, and displays its star-shaped flowers, yellow inside, and orange outside, in April. A flower for the tenacious garden lover, as it is difficult to grow in northern climates. It is about 8 in (20 cm) high. *T. kaufmanniana* (number 20) comes from the same regions. It flowers yellow-white to pale yellow in March. Its splended flowers are indispensable for every garden.

Below: Number 44:
'Toronto', a hybrid developed from
Tulipa greigii.

Above: Number 38: *Tulipa tarda.*

Number 43

Tulipa hoogiana has large, red to purple flowers, 10 in (25 cm) tall, suitable for the tulip lover who has dry soil and a sheltered position, or who has a glass-house with pots available.

Number 44

Tulipa greigii is found in the Chirchik valley of Turkmenistan where it is very striking with its orange colored flowers. The inside of the flower is yellow, and there is a black fleck on each petal. Height 10 in (25 cm).

Number 45

Tulipa fosteriana was discovered by Joseph Habenhauer in 1904 in the hills near Samarkand. It is identifiable by its striking bright red color. It will thrive in warm dry soil from March to early April. The 12 in (30 cm) high flowers and their stems and foliage are fully developed then. Splendid varieties, which are well worth collecting, have been selected by Dutch growers.

Right: Number 45:

Tulipa fosteriana **'Madame Lefebre'**

(syn. *T.f.* **'Red Emperor').**

Below: Number 6:

the single late tulip 'Queen of Night'.

Index

**Bolded page references
indicate photographs
Italicized names indicate a
Plant Family reference**